INDUSTRIALIZATION:

Brazil's Catalyst For Church Growth

INDUSTRIALIZATION:

Brazil's Catalyst
For Church Growth

a study of the RIO AREA
by c.w. gates

William Carey Library

533 HERMOSA STREET • SOUTH PASADENA, CALIF. 91030 • TEL. 213-682-2047

International Standard Book Number 0-87808-413-4
Library of Congress Catalog Number 72-81342

Published by the William Carey Library
533 Hermosa Street
South Pasadena, Calif. 91030
Telephone 213-682-2047

PRINTED IN THE UNITED STATES OF AMERICA

To

the faithful partners of God in Brazil--
missionaries, pastors, and laymen--who
are working together to realize a great
increase in the church of Jesus Christ

CONTENTS

FIGURES

ix

FOREWORD

"This carefully-documented study of Church growth in one
country may open the eyes of many readers to facts which will
revolutionize their thinking about the relation of Protestant
Christianity to the modern world. Too often we have assumed
that the forces which are rapidly and radically changing
society in the 'emergent' nations—urbanization, industrialization, and so forth—necessarily bring in their train a secular
way of thinking which can only be at odds with the Church.
This does not have to be the case! Charles Gates has shown
that these seismic social changes are also shaking millions
loose from encrusted traditional attitudes and making them open
as never before to experiencing the liberation and individuation
the Gospel gives. But to seize the opportunity will require
wisdom, understanding, and adaptability on the part of the
Church. This book will have a valuable role in updating our
thinking.

-Robert S. Ellwood, Jr.
Associate Professor of Religion
University of Southern California

Chapter 1
How the Action Began

The exciting relationship that exists between the grinding gears of Brazilian industry and the rapid growth of the Protestant church in Brazil is a captivating story. Industry in Brazil began to progress as the pressures of world civilization forced the nation from its traditional socio-cultural patterns of feudalism and latifundium. The Protestant church was able to penetrate the mores and life styles of the people after industrialization began to act upon the resistant colonial culture.

There is indication that the phenomena of industrialization and Protestantism existed parallel with each other from the middle years of the nineteenth century when they made their initial appearance in the Brazilian milieu. However, it was not until the worldwide crises of war and universal economic depression that they began to interact and exert forces of a revolutionary character upon the Brazilian culture.

Revolution is the only term sufficiently definitive to express the transformations that are occurring in the traditional Brazilian society. The society has been based upon two classes and an agricultural economy. The pervasive innovations of industrialization multiplies dramatically the contagion of revolution and the growth of the middle class.

The rise of industry and its concomitant causal effects upon the traditional culture of Brazil is contemporary history. Poppino writes:

> The rise of industry in Brazil after 1920 could not fail to encourage and reflect sweeping changes in the urban social structure and to effect the balance of political power between urban and rural areas . . . In the four decades ending in 1960 millions of migrants from the countryside swarmed into the cities drawn in part by the lure of jobs in shops, mills, and factories.[1]

Industrialization, since 1939, in Brazil has catapulted the nation into first place among Latin American nations

from an industrial viewpoint. The growth rate of industry
has been at 9.2 per cent per annum.[2]

Rapid industrial expansion, however, came after the second World War. Baklanoff states:

The phenomenal postwar economic expansion of Brazil was
substantially assisted by foreign capital participation,
particularly in the industrial sector which formed the
growing edge of the economy and in the financing of the
nation's economic infra-structure. Foreign capital flows
were especially decisive for Brazil after 1954 when the
coffee boom faded and the terms of trade affected the
economy adversely. In the period from 1947 to 1961
Brazil received more than 6.7 billion dollars in new
capital from foreign investment, comprising 1,438
million dollars in new venture capital (including an
estimated 607 million dollars in profits reinvested in
the country) and 5,262 million dollars in new loan capital.[3]

Protestantism was introduced into Brazil in 1855. The
first national census carried out in 1890 reported a total
of 143,743 Protestants after the first three decades of
growth. The Protestants represented one per cent of the
population. A second census was made in 1940. The total
number of Protestants had grown to 1,074,857 representing
2.61 per cent of the population. In 1950 a third census was
made reporting a total of 1,741,430 Protestants representing
3.35 per cent of the people of Brazil. The years between
1955 and 1960 report an increase of 492,264 members. The
growth rate is indicative of more than double that of the
general population.[4]

"The growth of the historical churches in Brazil has been
considerable since 1930."[5] The Baptists have maintained
their position of first place in membership gains. The
Presbyterians have continued in the second place. The Methodists have consistently held the third place among the historical denominations. The total Protestant membership for
the year 1966 was reported as 2,606,955.[6] The estimated
membership total for 1970 is 3,223,600.[7]

Most of the rapid Protestant growth has come in the
Pentecostal churches. These churches were introduced into
Brazil in 1911. The most spectacular growth rate has been
that of the Assemblies of God. The Assemblies have grown
from zero to 956,000 in a period of sixty years. William
Read has made an extensive study of the growth of the Protestant church in Brazil. Regarding the accelerated growth
of the Assemblies of God, he states:

From 1934 on, the yearly rate of increase has been about
23 per cent each year, 230 per cent each ten years!
Between 1934 and 1964 this Church has doubled its membership in less than five years several times.[8]

Technology and church growth are seemingly unrelated.
However, since the study made by Max Weber in the beginning
of the present century, technology and Protestantism have
been related subjects of extensive study. A starting point
in the research for this study was an analysis of the Web-
erian hypothesis which emphasizes the "connection of the
spirit of modern economic life with the rational ethics of
ascetic Protestantism."[9] An analysis of pertinent background material drawn from pre-industrial Brazil to modern
industrial Brazil is presented early in this study.

Three tools to help discover the relationship between
industrialization and church growth will be used during the
investigation. The first tool to be used is statistics
relating to the growth of industry and Protestant church
growth collected and computerized by the Missions Advanced
Research and Communication Center of Monrovia, California.
A second tool is that of a questionnaire mailed to respondents in the industrial belt of Brazil. This questionnaire
was structured in such a fashion that the items responded to
could be analyzed for illustration of the concomitant development of industrialization and Protestantism in Brazil
pointing out their combined socioeconomic effects upon
selected informants. The third tool is a series of interviews by recognized church growth authorities.

Emilio Willems of Vanderbilt University has made a
thoughtful and revealing study of the rise of Protestantism
in Brazil and Chile in his book, *Followers of the New
Faith*. His thesis was that Protestantism had its antece-
dents, if not its roots, in structural peculiarities of the
traditional Brazilian and Chilean societies.

During the course of his study Willems found that Protestantism was statistically strongest in industrialized and in
frontier areas. His research in Brazil was made in the São
Paulo area, both in the capital city and the state by the
same name. The São Paulo area is unquestionably the leader
in industrial production in Brazil. Likewise the largest
concentration of Protestants are found in the São Paulo
area.

This study comprises the industrial area of Rio de
Janeiro state. I am grateful for the impetus that Mr.
Willems has given by providing facts that bear out his
hypothesis of a relationship between the expansion of Protestantism and the emergence of an industrial society.

I have been an observer of the phenomena of industrialization and the rise of Protestantism in Brazil since 1958.
Industrialization and church growth are challenging reali-
ties in my personal experience as well as in the life of the
Church of Jesus Christ in Brazil.

NOTES

[1]Rollie E. Poppino, *Brazil, the Land and People* (London: Oxford University Press, 1968), p. 239.

[2]Jose Honorio Rodriques, *The Brazilians, Their Character and Aspirations* (Austin: University of Texas Press, 1968), p. 239.

[3]Eric N. Baklanoff, "Foreign Private Investment and Industrialization in Brazil," *New Perspectives of Brazil* (Nashville: Vanderbilt University Press, 1966), p. 102.

[4]Emilio Willems, *Followers of the New Faith* (Nashville: Vanderbilt University Press, 1967), pp. 66-67.

[5]*Ibid.*, p. 65.

[6]IBGE, *Anuário Estatístico do Brazil--1968* (Fundação IBGE, Instituto Brasileiro de Estatística, 1968), p. 487.

[7]"Continuing Evangelism in Brazil," *Missions Advanced Research and Communication Center*, An Interpretive Bulletin prepared by Missions Advanced Research and Communications Center (Monrovia: MARC/MIB, 1971), p. 12.

[8]William R. Read, *New Patterns of Church Growth in Brazil* (Grand Rapids: Wm. B. Eerdmans Publishing Co., 1965), p. 126.

[9]Max Weber, *The Protestant Ethic and the Spirit of Capitalism*, Trans. by Talcott Parsons (Charles Scribner's Sons, 1958), p. 292.

Chapter 2

The Land of a New Self-Image

Brazil was discovered by Pedro Alvares Cabral on April 22,
1500. Cabral was sailing with thirteen ships from Lisbon,
Portugal to the West Indies. His first view of the new land
was of a mountain. He named it Easter Mountain in honor of
the day of its discovery. Behind that mountain was a great
continent. The phrase, "Brazil is a continent,"[1] is used to
indicate the vastness, complexity, magnitude of its problems, accomplishments, and promise. The expression is
employed to create a vision of the unity that distinguishes
Brazil from Spanish America and from the recently independent countries of tropical Africa and Asia.

Poppino describes the present size of Brazil in clearly
understood terms:

> Brazil occupies approximately half of the continent of
> South America and accounts for one-third of the region
> known as Latin America. It covers 3,206,478 square
> miles, dwarfing the largest Spanish American Republics.
> Brazil has three times as much territory as Argentina and
> more than four times as much as Mexico; and it is larger
> than the continental United States by about 185,000
> square miles. Only China, the Soviet Union, and Canada
> surpass Brazil in contiguous land area.[2]

Brazil occupies the fourth place in the world in territorial
extent. It is nearly one hundred times that of Portugal.[3]

The Portuguese had discovered a tropical land, but one
that presented difficulties in the orographic context.
Vianna Moog when comparing the geography of Brazil with that
of the United States on its Eastern Seaboard found definite
contrasts. He pointed out that a visitor to the United
States would be impressed with the plains that would greet
him stretching from Miami to New York or from New York to
Philadelphia. The visitor would be surprised that there
were no granite parapets, tunnels, or viaducts. There would
be no mountains to blacken or erase the horizons. But it
would not be so in Brazil.[4] Moog writes:

What a contrast to the routes from Rio do Belo Horizonte, from Rio to Sao Paulo, from Paranagua to Curitiba, or from Sao Paulo to Santos! On them the plain is the exception; the rule is mountains, cliffs, tunnels, via-ducts, curves molded by the precipices of inhospitable mountain ranges.[5]

It is significant to recognize that modern highways are now leaping these natural obstacles to open and unite this vast country of opportunity.

What type of people were the colonizers of Brazil? How did they adapt to the tropical climate? What were the moti-vating forces that pushed them out from Europe? What were the attractions of the tropics that pulled these colonizers to the new world?

In 1494 the Treaty of Tordesillas divided the continent of South America between the Spanish and the Portuguese. The land of Brazil was divided into seventeen *capitanias*. These *capitanias* functioned for a century, for all practical purposes, as a separate colony with its own regional way of life. Maranhão, which in the seventeenth century extended to nearly all of the present northern area of Brazil, was officially linked directly to Portugal and not placed under the authority of Tomé de Souza, first governor of Brazil.[6]

Gilberto Freyre, Brazilian social historian, does not find a definite dynamic type in the Portuguese. The cus-toms, aspirations, interests, temperaments, vices, and virtues are a varied sort, and of diverse origins. There is a vagueness and lack of preciseness that permits the Portu-guese to unite within himself many contrasts.[7]

"It would be difficult to imagine a people more fluctu-ating than the Portuguese" who are able to maintain a balance of antagonisms.[8] These colonizers from the Iberian peninsula were not a simple extension of Europe into Brazil. Portugal is a conventially European state, but it is not orthodox in all its qualities, experiences, and conditions of life. It is in many respects a mixture of Europe and Africa, of Christianity and Islam. The Hispanic, or Iberian peninsula was dominated for eight centuries by the Africans. The understandable result was a leaving of traces of the Arabs and Moors on the culture of the people of the penin-sula. The result has been that the Portuguese are a people with a special capacity to maintain contradictions and even to harmonize them.[9]

The Portuguese were able to colonize Brazil because of their experience and cultural background. Only in Brazil has the white European been able to develop a society in the tropics. The Brazilian society has been called a "cultural mosaic" of three elements, the Lusitanian, Indian, and Afri-can. Both the African and Indian traits have survived to contribute much to Brazilian national culture. However, there was not a fusion of traditions, but rather a welding of the African and American-Indian traits into an essentially Luso-Brazilian culture. The Portuguese, Catholic, aristocratic masters were the cultural models for the African slave, the American Indian, and the mixed descendents of the colonizers with these races.[10]

The Portuguese, being the dominant group, were able to impose their European culture on the slaves and Indians. It is normal to expect that this pattern was not unilateral. However, there was a process of acculturation. The Indians and Africans did exert a strong influence upon their European masters. Along with these dual influences, there was the third influence of the exotic force of the new climate to be found in their New World.

The Portuguese colonizers were the generating force of an entirely original type of society that was being developed in the tropics. The original simple commercial trading station was an impossibility, but the society did maintain a pronounced mercantile character about it. The new society was based on the enterprise of the white colonist. He brought labor to the new land and recruited labor among the races that he dominated in the tropics. There was an adaptation of the traditional commercial objective to meet new conditions. An agricultural society was formed, based on the production of sugar cane to supply the demands of the European nobility.[11] Regarding this new society, Gilberto Freyre states:

In any event, it is a known fact that the Portuguese triumphed where other Europeans failed; and the first modern society formed in the tropics with national characteristics and qualities was one of the Portuguese origin. These were qualities that in Brazil came early instead of late as in the tropical possessions of the English, the French, and the Dutch.[12]

The Portuguese colonizers were aided by their native miscibility and mobility in the conquest of the new land.[13] Miscibility rather than mobility was the process by which the colonizers made up their deficiency for volumes and human mass in the colonizations of extensive areas. Their own land had been occupied by those who were of a darker pigmentation. The Mohammedans were more highly skilled and possessed an intellectual culture superior to that of the blond Christians of the peninsula. Thus the Portuguese had been prepared for this kind of colonization.[14]

There was another quality enjoyed by the Portuguese which aided them in their efforts to subdue and conquer. It was that of acclimatability. The Northern Europeans were unable to establish an all-white society in the tropics. The French Calvinists had attempted this in the sixteenth century in the Rio de Janeiro area. They retired from the colonizing scene without leaving even a trace of their efforts. The tropics worked toward the degeneration of the white colonizers. The Portuguese found it possible to adapt. It was through hybridization that the Portuguese really succeeded in colonizing Brazil. A mixed population overcame the adverse conditions of the climate.[15]

Poppino states:

> It is apparent that the process of acculturation and racial mixture that was eventually to give rise to a distinctive Brazilian society had begun well before the turn of the seventeenth century.[16]

Comparisons between the colonization of the United States and the colonization of Brazil are generally considered in an overall view of the progress of the countries. There has been an outstanding attempt made to compare the colonizing of the two giants by the noted Brazilian sociologist, Vianna Moog. He has seriously considered the lands and the people involved in their role of colonizers. He attempts to answer clearly why it is that Brazil is a developing nation, while the United States of America has developed so completely. Moog states:

> There is of course a fundamental difference of motives in the settlement of the two countries: an initially spiritual, practical, and constructive spirit in the development of North America, and a predatory, extractive and almost secondarily religious spirit in the development of Brazil.[17]

The facts of history show that there were other pull factors influencing the Puritans of the *Mayflower* to the New World than the attraction of gold and silver mines and prospects of easy riches. There were pushing factors that caused them to move out. Persecution at home forced them out "in search of lands where they could worship their God, read and interpret their Bible, work, help one another and celebrate the ritual of their cult in their own way."[18]

The North American colonizers were not sent out by a monarch to bring back riches. The Puritans took their families with them. They embarked without looking back. They were going out to found a new fatherland with no thought of returning to their country of origin. The Puritans of colonizers, not conquerors. The sense, the rhythm of North American history was already definitely established--constructive, moral, practical.[19]

In contrast to the Puritans of North American colonizing a new land, in Brazil, unfortunately, the contrary occurred in nearly everything. These men were sent out by the King of Portugal with a purpose of finding and extracting wealth from the New World. They were not family men. Furthermore, they were not devoted to work as a source of gaining wealth.[20] Poppino states:

From the arrival of the first Europeans on the shores of Brazil, sporadic probes were made through the barriers of forest and mountain in search of fabled Indian treasures like those the Spanish encountered in Mexico and Peru.[21]

Another contrast between the colonizers of North America and the Portuguese of Brazil was the fact that the idea of remaining in the New World was foreign to the Portuguese colonizers. In the seventeenth century, "the *bandeirante* always advanced, but with an eye on his point of departure.[22]

The Portuguese *bandeirante* was not as fortunate in achieving his goal of finding gold and silver to carry back to his sovereign, as was his Spanish counterpart in the regions now known as Spanish America. Eventually there was discovered and appreciated the Brazil wood, "Pau Brasil," for its qualities of red dye for the textile industry of Europe. When the conquistador recognized the frustration of his plans of simply finding wealth, "the Portuguese became agriculturists out of necessity."[23] In order to realize their desires of acquiring wealth, and in order to defend their possession of Brazil, the Portuguese turned to the land and built up great sugar plantations. This was primarily realized in the Northeast region of the colony.

It was in this turning to agriculture that the cultural pattern of Brazil was formed that endured for three centuries. The "Casa Grande" was the large plantation house built by the barons to stand through the centuries. The feudal pattern of social and commercial life was struck with the turning to the land. The Casa Grande dominated everything, even the Church. Gilberto Freyre states:

The Big House in Brazil, in the impulse that it manifested from the very start to be the mistress of the land, overcame the church. It overcame the Jesuit as well, leaving the lord of the manor as almost the sole dominating figure in the colony. The true lord of Brazil, . . . but all this pomp has long since turned to dust, and when all is said, it was the church that survived the Big Houses.[24]

The Portuguese were dominating the New World of the tropics as plantation owners and not as seekers after mineral wealth. Labor was needed to produce the sugar cane. Slavery was the recourse that was opted by the landholders. Slavery was the most important organization of the colonial period. However, it did not provide a superstructure for lasting and meaningful social relations. Prado states:

Slave labor progressed no further than its original point of departure, compulsory physical effort. It provided no training or preparation for a higher plane of human existence. It contributed no moral element to these social relationships, on the contrary, it led to

the degradation of the slaves and any cultural content he
might have brought with him from his original state was
obliterated. The master-slave relationship was and
remained a purely material one, centered on labor and
production and added little or nothing to the colony's
cultural complex.[25]

What type of personality was established in the New World
of the tropics? What was the racial makeup of the Brazilian? What did this "new man" have as an image of himself?
Was his understanding a dynamic or a static concept? Did
the ruling class differ substantially in his understanding
of himself from that of the slave or serf population? How
did the Brazilian feel about his relationships to his family
and to his religion? Who were the Brazilians? Who are the
Brazilians?

The outstanding North American authority on Brazil,
T. Lynn Smith, writes:

A thorough study of the racial make-up of the Brazilian
population and of the manner in which the various elements are distributed among the regions and classes of
the country would in itself be a life's work. If the
United States is described as a "melting pot," Brazil
must be considered a caldron. No other country has had
for four hundred years such large numbers of white, red,
and black people thrown into so close physical and social
contact with one another. To the already extremely
heterogeneous population, composed of these three original strains and of which the white Portuguese component
was already a composite of many elements, the nineteenth
and twentieth centuries brought millions of Europeans,
mainly Italians, Germans, Poles, Portuguese, and
Spaniards, and the twentieth century has added large
contingents of Lebanese and Japanese.[26]

The main current of immigration to Brazil began in 1887.
A trickle of Portuguese arrived as early as 1874. The five
principal nationalities represented in the influx of immi-
grants between the years 1884 and 1957, according to the
statistics presented by T. Lynn Smith, were: Italy with
1,510,078; Portugal with 1,457,617; Spain with 657,744;
Japan with 209,184; and Germany with 192,574.[27]

These figures are indicative of the pattern which was in
progress from the earliest colonial times until the present.
Rodriques credits Karl Friedrich Philips, a Bavarian botan-
ist who visited Brazil in the years 1817-1820, as the earliest student of Brazil, who appreciated the fact that the
unique quality of Brazil's population was derived from its
cultural fusion. This fusion is still in progress. The key
to understanding Brazil is in the amalgamation of the
races.[28]

Finding this key to understanding Brazil, however, did not change the attitude of the colonial society and of the Brazilian who lived in a condition of inertia for three hundred years. Prado writes:

"The colonial population was apathetic even in its pleasures and pastimes." The atmosphere in which the colonial population moved, or rather, "rested", was contaminated by a virus of laziness and lassitude, which infected all but a few. Brazil was the picture of stagnation.[29]

It was a sad panorama offered by colonial society. It may be summarized as a scattered and unstable settlement, with an economy which was poor and miserable, whose mores were dissolute, and whose administration, lay and ecclesiastical, was inept and corrupt.[30] This feudal society was the soil from which grew the image of the uselessness and unworthwhileness of the Brazilian even in his self-image. He developed into a usually patient, forebearing, docile individual through the sufferings and humiliations he received from the masters.

There developed a feeling of worthlessness among the Brazilians. They developed what Gilberto Freyre termed the feeling of a mongrel people because of their mixture of the races.

Many factors have contributed to change the image of the Brazilian from the mixed, mongrel "complex" to one of pride in his heritage and to the self-image of a "universal" people with something to be proud of and to share with the world community.

High among these influences of the nineteenth century was the abolition of slavery without the horror of civil war. The greatest influence of the twentieth century was the feeling of accomplishment and value that was injected into the Brazilian's self-image with the building of the new national capital, Brasília, on the high plateau seven hundred miles inland from Rio de Janeiro. Another factor has been the writings of their own Brazilian sociologists, such as Vianna Moog, who has written to explode what he terms "the myth of the racial superiority of the Anglo-Saxons."[31]

The Brazilians have suffered for a long time from what many term a national inferiority complex. It is only in the present generation that the values of the national culture are becoming values of pride. The anxiety concerning miscegenation and the theories of some who would doom the Brazilian as an inferior people began to change almost imperceptibly. The change had been in the embryonic stage for many years before World War II, but it was not until after the war that the Brazilians viewed their country with real pride. This pride has taken on many forms including pride in the national industry, the selection of Miss Brazil, tourism, and the national pride in their tri-champion world soccer team.[32]   The Brazilian self-image today is new and beautiful.

We turn now to a consideration of the Brazilian family and to the religions of the country.

NOTES

[1]Poppino, *op. cit.*, p. 9.

[2]*Ibid.*

[3]Potsch, *op. cit.*, p. 37.

[4]Vianna Moog, *Bandeirantes and Pioneers*, Trans. by L. L. Barrett (New York: George Braziller, 1969), p. 17.

[5]*Ibid.*

[6]Charles Wagley, *An Introduction to Brazil* (New York: Columbia University Press, 1963), p. 28.

[7]Gilberto Freyre, *The Masters and the Slaves* (New York: Knopf, 1956), p. 16.

[8]*Ibid.*

[9]Gilberto Freyre, *New World in the Tropics* (New York: Knopf, 1959), pp. 39-41.

[10]Wagley, *op. cit.*, p. 9.

[11]Caio Prado, Jr., *The Colonial Background of Modern Brazil*, Trans. by Suzette Macedo (Berkeley: University of California Press, 1969), p. 20.

[12]Freyre, *The Masters and the Slaves*, p. 23.

[13]*Ibid.*, p. 21.

[14]*Ibid.*, p. 19.

[15]*Ibid.*, pp. 23-24.

[16]Poppino, *op. cit.*, p. 67.

[17]Moog, *op. cit.*, p. 92.

[18]*Ibid.*

[19]*Ibid.*

[20]*Ibid.*, p. 95.

[21] Poppino, p. 68.

[22] *Ibid.*, p. 176.

[23] Freyre, *The Masters and the Slaves*, p. 39.

[24] *Ibid.*, p. 8.

[25] Prado, *op. cit.*, p. 401.

[26] T. Lynn Smith, *Brazil, People and Institutions* (Baton Rouge: Louisiana State University Press, 1963), p. 51.

[27] *Ibid.*, pp. 118-122.

[28] Rodriques, *op. cit.*, pp. vii-viii.

[29] Prado, *op. cit.*, p. 408.

[30] *Ibid.*, p. 414.

[31] Freyre, *The Masters and the Slaves*.

[32] Wagley, *op. cit.*, pp. 268-275.

Chapter 3

Major Religions of Brazil

The family is the primary social relationship in Brazil. "The large, aristocratic, patriarchal family always has been the most important of Brazil's social institutions."[1] Azevedo states:

> The family, was beyond any doubt, the main basis of Brazilian society: it provided for our juridical institutions, our patriarchal paternalism, our ethic realism, our domestic particularism in religion, in politics, and in business; also for much of our art, of our tastes, or our psychology. From that basic familism derives our peculiar individualism, or rather our privatism. Nevertheless, the role of historical circumstances and of our structural and situational factors which support types of unions deviating from the traditional archtype deserves more consideration.[2]

The social stratification of Brazil is the structure from which choice of mates and the organization of the family takes place. This has been the pattern from the colonial period and the traditional feudal system of latifundium.

Brazil could possibly be generalized in its social stratification as a two-class society. This would have been more accurate during the colonial and imperial phases of the nation's history. There has been, however, a class that would fit the pattern of middle class, especially from the time of the empire. The main groupings that comprise the Brazilian people at the present according to Azevedo are three:

> . . . an upper class, or the elite, a middle class, and a lower class, the first is more or less on the same footing as the old estate of rich whites: it includes most of those pheno-typically Europoid and socially "white" of the traditional families, the descendents of the old aristocracy, the leading businessmen, bankers, industrialists, professionals, and civil officers. The middle class includes all the whites and *mestiços* of the professions, the nonmanual activities. Identification with the

values, aspirations, and privileges of the elite is a
trait of the culture of the middle sector. It thus hap-
pens that through their mutual identification and assimi-
lation, these two groups still coalesce in a "superior"
stratum within whose boundaries there prevails a maximum
of circulation through vertical mobility and inter-
marriage. The "inferior" group coincides with the lower
class, comprising the Negroes, the *mesticos*, and some
whites of the lowest economic levels and manual
occupations.[3]

The large families or *parentelas* of colonial Brazil have
continued into the present day. "Brazilians used to be first
members of a family, then of a region, and finally of their
nation; now I would say that they are Brazilians first, but
they never forget their family connections."[4] Opportunity
for continued church growth is found by reaching into the
close relationships of the Brazilian families.

Religion is important in Brazil. Roman Catholicism was
introduced at the time of its conquest. Today, Brazil is
the largest Roman Catholic nation in the world. However,
the masses of the Brazilians have a nominal relationship to
the church. Willems describes the variation in the relationship as a "habit of classifying oneself as 'Catholic,'
whether pious or lax, agnostic or openly anticlerical."[5]

Religion dominated the life styles of the Brazilian in
the colonial period. In matter of fact, Roman Catholicism
was the official religion of the nation. Freyre considered
Catholicism in colonial Brazil as "the cement"[6] of the unity
of the country. Prado, however, considered it "no more than
a skeleton draped in the outward pomp of rites and cere-
monies, devoid of all higher feelings."[7]

Roman Catholicism continued to be the religion of the
country during the period of the empire. Smith states:

There was a freedom of religion and worship in Brazil
that contrasted sharply with the severe restraints
imposed in Spanish America. With the declaration of the
republic in 1889 and the adoption of the constitution of
1890 there was a separation of church and state and the
official establishment of full freedom of religion.[8]

Most of the practicing Catholics are found in the urban
areas. The 1950 census registered 93.5 per cent of the
Brazilian population as Roman Catholics.[9] However, not more
than ten per cent are in attendance at mass on a given Sunday. The large percentage of non-practicing Catholics are
probably found among the peasantry. It is in this extensive
mass of the population that "folk-Catholicism" is found.
Willems states:

The Latin American peasantry is not irreligious nor anti-
religious. Much on the contrary, its culture is

saturated with religious beliefs and practices reflecting
intimate and rather pragmatic relationships to all sorts
of events and life crises that the individual feels he
cannot control except by recourse to the supernatural.
The core institution of Latin American "folk Catholicism"
is undoubtedly the cult of the saints. All other institutions, particularly the brotherhoods, novenas, fiestas,
pilgrimages, and street processions revolve around the
cult of the saints, the nature of which clashes with
official Catholic doctrine.[10]

Another form of religion which thousands of Brazilians
follow is the traditional African fetish cults. These were
brought to Brazil by the slaves, reinterpreted and now
flourish throughout Brazil. They have various names according to the region of the country. The name of *candomblé*
used in Bahia; *macumba* is used in Rio de Janeiro. The cults
are fused with Catholicism and most of the adepts consider
themselves Catholics.[11]

Spiritist worship is also a flourishing religion in
Brazil. There is a division in this between the "high" and
the "low." "The doctrinal writings on 'Spiritism' by the
Frenchman Allan Kardec have been accepted in Brazil as a
rich system of science, philosophy, and religion."[12] The
census of 1966 reports a total of 758,209 Kardec members,
and 185,442 members of the "low" spiritism known as
Umbanda.[13]

Protestantism was first introduced into Brazil on a per-
manent basis by the Lutherans who immigrated to Brazil from
Germany in 1823. The first settlements of the Lutherans
were in São Paulo and Rio de Janeiro. The first Protestant
church was that of the Lutheran denomination, organized in
Rio de Janeiro in 1837.[14] The Lutherans soon settled in the
southern part of Brazil, but demonstrated little interest in
the dissemination of the Protestant creed. Willems states:

> These largely German-speaking settlers not only confined
> themselves to certain areas but were also committed to a
> self-imposed blend of nationalistic and religious values.
> The Prussian Evangelical Church succeeded in transfering
> to Latin America the idea that *Deutschtum* and the Gospel
> depended upon each other for survival. . . . These self-
> imposed restrictions prevented these churches from devel-
> oping the very kind of religious proselytism which char-
> acterizes other brands of Protestantism in Latin
> America.[15]

The French Hugenots attempted to establish a haven from
persecution in the area of Rio de Janeiro in the 1550's. It
was also to be a base for evangelization of the Indians.
The Dutch also attempted to introduce Protestantism during
their thirty-year control over northern Brazil. They likewise were repulsed by the Portuguese.[16] These attempts were
not successful in introducing Protestantism into Brazil.

However, the Huguenots did have a signal honor which is not generally known. Kidder states:

> How few Protestants are cognizant of the fact that in the terri-
> tory of Brazil the Reformed Religion was first proclaimed on the
> Western Continent! [17]

It was not until 1855, with the arrival of Robert Reid Kalley, that Protestantism took root and began to grow. Kalley had been a missionary to the Madeira Islands before his arrival in Brazil. He was a medical doctor who combined evangelism with medicine. The zeal of this Scotch Presbyterian missionary was such that he was successful in organizing churches in Niterói, Rio de Janeiro, and Pernambuco in the northeast before terminating his work in 1876. [18]

This successful beginning of the Protestant church in Brazil was soon followed by the historical denominations. Presbyterian missionaries from the northern branch of the Presbyterian Church in the United States arrived in 1859. The missionaries from the southern branch of the Presbyterian church arrived in 1869. The Methodists were the next to arrive in the year 1880. The Southern Baptists sent their pioneer missionaries in 1881. The Episcopalians entered in 1889. [19]

The Assembly of God was the first of the Pentecostal churches to enter Brazil. Their first two missionaries, Gunnar Vingren and Daniel Berg, entered Belem in 1910. The church became an indigenous church and has grown with great rapidity. The present membership is approximately 1,000,000.

Another of the Pentecostal churches that has had an accelerated rate of growth is the Congregaçao Crista. This church was introduced into Brazil in 1910 by Louis Francescon, a missionary of Italian descent from Chicago. The church membership is 500,000. [20]

It is primarily from these two churches that the accelerated Protestant growth has come in Brazil.

NOTES

[1] Smith, *op. cit.*, p. 459.

[2] Thales de Azevedo, *Social Change in Brazil* (Gainesville: University of Florida Press, 1963), pp. 5-6.

[3] *Ibid.*

[4] Wagley, *op. cit.*, p. 204.

[5] Willems, *op. cit.*, p. vi.

[6] Freyre, *The Masters and the Slaves*, p. 45.

[7] Prado, *op. cit.*, p. 414.

[8] Smith, *op. cit.*, p. 510.

[9] *Ibid.*, p. 511.

[10] Willems, *op. cit.*, p. 35.

[11] Wagley, *op. cit.*, p. 511.

[12] Read, *op. cit.*, p. 210.

[13] IBGE *Anuario Estatísticas--1966*, p. 488.

[14] MARC, *Interpretive Bulletin* (Monrovia: MARC), p. 9.

[15] Willems, *op. cit.*, p. 210.

[16] William R. Read, Victor M. Monterroso, Harmon A. Johnson, *Latin American Church Growth* (Grand Rapids: Wm. B. Eerdmans Publishing Co., 1969), p. 36.

[17] D. P. Kidder and J. C. Fletcher, *Brazil and the Brazilians* (New York: Childs and Peterson, 1857), p. 4.

[18] Read, Monterroso, Johnson, *op. cit.*, p. 39.

[19] Read, *op. cit.*,,pp. 121-122.

[20] MARC, Bulletin I, p. 19.

Chapter 4

Dynamic Church Growth in the Rio Area

Brazilian industrialization cam be divided into two periods
for convenience, that of the "Old Republic" and that of the
"New Republic." The first period extended from the time of
the establishment of the Republic in 1889 to the period of
the beginning of the dictatorship in 1930 under Getúlio
Vargas. The second period extends from 1930 until the
present.

Coffee was the chief product during this period. From
Rio de Janeiro to São Paulo and even on to the new lands of
the state of Paraná, the coffee barons with their *fazendas*
and city palaces were the holders of the Nation's capital.
The railroads, which were important in the early phases of
the development of industry, were being constructed to
transport the coffee into São Paulo and on to the port of
Santos for export. After 1910, it was the railroads coming
into São Paulo that helped develop it into the major industrial center of the nation.[1] World War I stimulated the
industry of the São Paulo complex to furnish foods and
textiles for other regions of the country.

During the "Old Republic" phase, the absence of heavy and
basic industries was one of the greatest obstacles to industrial evolution in Brazil. Iron ore was readily available
in the area of Belo Horizonte, but the coal necessary for
the furnaces was of poor quality and far to the south in the
state of Santa Caterina. This lack of fuel retarded the
progress of industrialization in Brazil during the first
decades of the twentieth century.[2]

The "Old Republic" period of industrialization was an era
of limited industrial growth. There were some factors, however, that promoted industrialization. Azevedo states:

The industry of the nation which under the Empire only
began to become significant after 1885, in spite of
various earlier efforts to implant industry in Brazil,
had no growth until the twentieth century, when it was
favored by a combination of factors, some of them related
to the rise of coffee on the plateau, and others result-

19

ing from the repercussions of the war of 1914 in the
Brazilian Market.[3]

Until "the first years after the Second World War, Brazil
was still primarily an agricultural country, heavily
dependent on its traditional exports, mainly coffee, cocoa,
cotton, and sugar.[4]   The Brazilian society was still the
traditional society of Freyre's *Casa Grande*.

The world depression of the thirties and the Paulist
Rebellion of 1931, apparently had ended a half-century of
economic prosperity during which time coffee from Brazil had
cornered the world market.   "The price of coffee dropped
from 24.8 cents per pound in March of 1929 to 7.6 cents in
October of 1931."[5]   The Vargas government protected the
planters by stockpiling the coffee.   The fortunes earned
through the coffee boom were thus conserved for investment.
The Brazilians turned their attention to national industry
when they were unable to purchase consumer items from the
world market during the depression.[6]   As a result the
industrialization of the "New Republic" began to emerge.

The usual cycle of economy in Brazil has been that of an
economic boom followed by a period of decadence.   This
occurred with the sugar industry, the gold mining, the rubber boom and would have occurred with the coffee if the
state of São Paulo had not changed its method of agriculture
and invested its resources in industry.   Wagley emphasizes
this by stating:

The next great economic cycle was industrial.   Beginning
in the 1930s, the area around and between Rio de Janeiro
and São Paulo slowly became Brazil's industrial center.
São Paulo was its heart, and today it is perhaps the
world's fastest-growing industrial area.   Industry
brought urban development and the growth of universities
and scientific institutions.   Industrial cities called
for modern communications and attracted a cosmopolitan
population.[7]

The thirties were the background for industrialization in
the "New Republic."   The rapid industrialization began following World War II.   Baer states:

As measured in 1947 constant prices, the share of agriculture in the gross domestic product declined from 27 percent in 1947 to 22 percent in 1961, while the share of
industry increased during the same period from 21 percent
to 34 percent.   During that period Brazil experienced one
of the highest real growth rates in Latin America, the
growth of the real gross domestic product averaging almost
6 percent per year, reaching 7.7 percent in 1961.[8]

Industrialization in Brazil was slowed down in the sixties as a result of spiraling inflation and communism
pressing upon the people which finally erupted in the

Revolution of March 31, 1964.

The editors of *Business Week* stated:

Brazil's inflation seemed unstoppable for decades. It
swelled to a 144% annual rate for a while in the early
1960s and almost wrecked the Brazilian economy. To stop
the inflation, the military government that took over in
1964 applied conventional remedies of economic austerity
which practically halted business expansion.

Now Brazilians have learned to live with a controlled
inflation and business is booming again. The sprawling
Latin giant has had two years of 9% growth--on top of a
19% price inflation last year--and gross national product
has climbed to $35 billion. It looks as if 1971 will be
just as good.[9]

The industrialization of the forties and fifties was
spurred on by the national steel industry and the buildup of
the automobile industry. These were basic industries for
continual growth. The market for the surge of industrial
products has been expanded by the construction of Brasilia
and the new highways system that are linking the "empty"
boxcars with the "locomotive" of industrialization. This is
to use the figure often employed by the Brazilians representing São Paulo as the industrial locomotive pulling the
train of empty and preindustrial states comprising the "New
Republic."

This figure of speech is no longer as descriptive of
Brazil as it once was. Industrialization is developing in
regions throughout Brazil. The Industrial Center of Aratú
is being constructed just fifteen kilometers from Salvador,
the capital city of Bahia in the northeast of Brazil. This
area of the nation and the state of Bahia, in particular, is
famous for holding onto the traditional values of the Brazilian culture. In the current year, Cr$2,600,000,000
(US $520,000,000) will be invested in one hundred thirty
project related to Aratú. This industrial center is the
first planned industrial center in Latin America. Light,
medium, and heavy industry has already been installed in the
center. The first residential unit of eight hundred houses
for workers has been constructed. The houses have been sold
on long-term financing.[10]

Industrialization in Brazil has been analyzed in terms of
decades. The forties was its entry into the steel age, the
fifties saw Brazil become a member of the oil community, the
sixties saw the maturing of the automotive industry, and in
the seventies, Brazil will enter the technological era.[11]

Problems of employment are facing Brazil with a mass of
seven million more young people coming into the fifteen to
twenty age group. A million new jobs a year are needed to
absorb those who have reached eighteen years of age.[12]

Brazil has entered the mainstream of contemporary civilization. It has become a part of a world that is transforming itself. Brazil is entering the future described by Joseph Kahl as one

which tends to unify all nations through similar themes: the pursuit of a high standard of living through industrial modes of production utilizing advanced technology; the organization of large-scale social units for efficient production and distribution, and for execution of public tasks.[13]

Industrialization and its consequences in Brazil are being reflected throughout every fiber of its changing culture.

Brazil is booming. Industrial production is continually climbing. As advances are made in technological progress, the opportunity for rapid church growth continues to rise. This is evident in the area surrounding Rio de Janeiro.

We shall consider the dynamic church growth of the Rio area as it is presented in available Brazilian government statistics relating to industrial production and Protestant church membership. The city of Rio de Janeiro will not be included in the study. The city of Rio de Janeiro composes the state of Guanabara. However, the dynamic influence of the city is easily recognizable in the growth of industry and in the adjacent counties of the state of Rio de Janeiro.

There are sixty-three counties (*municípios*) in the state of Rio de Janeiro. Sixteen of the counties have a production value of Cr$1,000,000,000 or above, according to the statistics presented by the Serviço Nacional de Recenseamento (National Survey Service) in its industrial atlas published in 1965.[14] The county of Volta Redonda had the highest production value with a total of Cr$19,804,000,000. Barra Mansa was second with production value of Cr$7,602,-000,000. Third in the descending scale was Duque de Caxias with Cr$6,141,000,000. The fourth in production value was the county of Niterói with Cr$5,417,000,000. Fifth was the county of Petrópolis with a value of Cr$5,256,000,000. Sixth was the county of Nova Iguaçu with production value of Cr$5,216,000,000. Seventh was the county of São Gonçalo with a value of Cr$4,949,000,000. Campos is the seventh county in the descending scale having had production value of Cr$4,554,000,000. The remainder of the sixteen counties had an inferior amount to Cr$2,000,000,000, but at least Cr$1,000,000,000.[15]

The Protestant church statistics for the state of Rio de Janeiro are collected in the *Estatística do Culto Protestante do Brasil*. The statistics for the years of 1959 and 1960 have been a special study of the MARC-MIB research team. This team of technicians has taken advantage of the modern means of technology to computerize the statistics. Their findings reveal the rate of church growth by categories of denominations for each county of the state for 1959 and 1960. The total church growth rate for each county is also presented in the read-outs.

The categories are as follows: Category I includes churches or denominations defined as traditional denominational groups such as Lutherans, Presbyterians, Methodists, Congregationalists, Episcopalians, and Baptists; Category II includes churches or sects defined as Pentecostal such as the Assembly of God; and Category III includes Marginal Sects such as the Seventh-Day Adventist, Jehovah Witnesses, and The Church of Latter-Day Saints of Jesus Christ.[16] Marginal sects are classified as Protestants by the Brazilian government for statistical purposes. However, the groups are not considered a participating part of the body of Protestant denominations in Brazil.

The sixteen counties of the state of Rio de Janeiro which had the highest Protestant membership for the year 1959, are scaled from the highest to the lowest as follows: Nova Iguaçu, 12,171; Campos, 11,481; Duque de Caxias, 9,910; Niterói, 9,184; Petrópolis, 6,702; Itaperuna, 4,332; Santo Antônio de Pádua, 3,115; Magé, 2,666; São Gonçalo, 2,621; Itaguaí, 2,610; Nilópolis, 2,593; Nova Friburgo, 2,449; Cabo Frio, 2,306; Volta Redonda, 2,301; Macaé, 2,077; and São Fidelis, 1,886.

The outstanding growth rate according to the percentages of the total number of categories was that of Macaé. The county had a total increase of 28.31%. This is 20% above the rate which the MARC-MIB group consider excellent growth. The highest percentage growths, according to the categories, indicate Macaé in Category I with 38.34%; Campos in Category II with 16.87%; and Nova Friburgo in Category III with 78.95%.

Category I shows seven of the counties with 8% growth or above. Category II indicates seven counties with 8% growth or above. All counties of the sixteen highest in membership have churches in Category I; thirteen counties have churches in Category II; eight counties have churches in Category III.

Outstanding percentage growth of the churches of Category II, which are the Pentecostal groups, are recorded in the first five counties, according to membership. The range is from 11.69% to 16.87%. Only Duque de Caxias has shown remarkable growth in these top five counties in Category I. Two of the five show minus growth rate; one shows less than one per cent and the fourth shows only 3.01%. In these same five counties the churches of Category III have poor growth rate except in Niterói where a record growth of 41.53% is reported. This seems to indicate a pattern of high percentage growth among the churches of Category II in the counties of highest industrial production, with a pattern of poor percentage growth in the Category I churches.

The 1960 statistics of the sixteen counties with highest Protestant membership show minor changes from those of 1959. Niterói assumed third place while Duque de Caxias fell to fourth place. Itaperuna showed a marked decrease in membership, falling from sixth to eleventh position. The county of Itaperuna showed a total percentage loss of 36.43%. These losses were nearly equally divided between the Category I group with 34.86% and Category II with 38.37%. There has been a migration of 20% from the rural areas in this microregion.[17] Another loss is seen in the county of Nilópolis which fell from eleventh position to fifteenth place. Its losses were in both Category I, with 5.76%, and in Category II with 3.48%. Category III continued to show a good growth of 8.45%. The decrease could be a result of the physical limitations of Nilópolis and the pull of larger industrialized counties in the immediate area such as Duque de Caxias.

Figures 1 and 2, which follow, present a comparison of the sixteen counties in the state of Rio de Janeiro with the highest industrial production and largest Protestant church membership for the years 1959 and 1960, respectively. Ten of the counties are in both columns indicating the high correlation of industrialization and growth of the Protestant church.

Figure 3 presents the sixteen most highly industrialized counties in 1959, within their respective microregions. Figure 4 presents the sixteen counties with the highest Protestant church membership in 1959.

Figure 5 indicates the ten counties which are shown in both Figures 3 and 4. Seven of the counties are in the Micro-Region 221.

The estimated population for the state of Rio de Janeiro for 1965 was 4,027,000 inhabitants. The estimated population for the micro-Region 221 was 1,861,612. This represents 46.23% of the population of the state in Micro-Region 221.

The total Protestant church membership for the state of Rio de Janeiro for 1965 was 163,118.[18] Micro-Region 221 had 43.68% of the state's Protestant population. However, 84.1% of the Protestants of the Micro-Region reside in the six counties of the region which are indicated in Figures 1 and 2 as having a production value of Cr$1,000,000,000. These six are the counties of Duque de Caxias, Magé, Nova Iguaçu, Nilópolis, Niterói, and São Gonçalo. These six have a total of 59,925 of the 71,245 Protestants in the Micro-Region. Of these members, 53.67% are among the Category II groups. The remaining six counties have a combined total of 11,320, which is 15.9% of the total.

47254

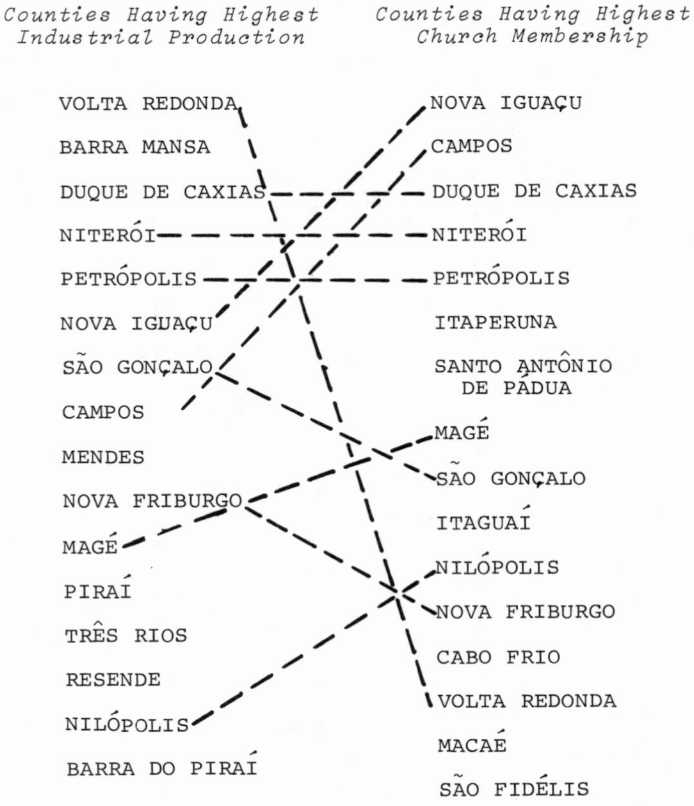

Counties Having Highest Industrial Production	Counties Having Highest Church Membership

```
VOLTA REDONDA          NOVA IGUAÇU

BARRA MANSA            CAMPOS

DUQUE DE CAXIAS        DUQUE DE CAXIAS

NITERÓI                NITERÓI

PETRÓPOLIS             PETRÓPOLIS

NOVA IGUAÇU            ITAPERUNA

SÃO GONÇALO            SANTO ANTÔNIO
                         DE PÁDUA

CAMPOS                 MAGÉ

MENDES                 SÃO GONÇALO

NOVA FRIBURGO          ITAGUAÍ

MAGÉ                   NILÓPOLIS

PIRAÍ                  NOVA FRIBURGO

TRÊS RIOS              CABO FRIO

RESENDE                VOLTA REDONDA

NILÓPOLIS              MACAÉ

BARRA DO PIRAÍ         SÃO FIDÉLIS
```

Fig. 1.--Comparison of 16 counties of the state of Rio de Janeiro having highest industrial production levels with 16 counties of the same state with highest levels of Protestant church membership for the year of 1959.

Counties Having Highest Industrial Production	Counties Having Highest Church Membership
VOLTA REDONDA	NOVA IGUAÇU
BARRA MANSA	CAMPOS
DUQUE DE CAXIAS	NITERÓI
NITERÓI	DUQUE DE CAXIAS
PETRÓPOLIS	PETRÓPOLIS
NOVA IGUAÇU	SAO GONÇALO
SÃO GONÇALO	SANTO ANTÔNIO DE PÁDUA
CAMPOS	ITAGUAÍ
MENDES	NOVA FRIBURGO
NOVA FRIBURGO	MAGÉ
MAGÉ	ITAPERUNA
PIRAÍ	CABO FRIO
TRÊS RIOS	VOLTA REDONDA
RESENDE	MACAÉ
NILOPOLIS	NILÓPOLIS
BARRA DO PIRAÍ	SÃO FIDÉLIS

Fig. 2.--Comparison of 16 counties of the state of Rio de Janeiro having highest industrial production levels with 16 counties of the same state with highest levels of Protestant church membership for the year of 1960.

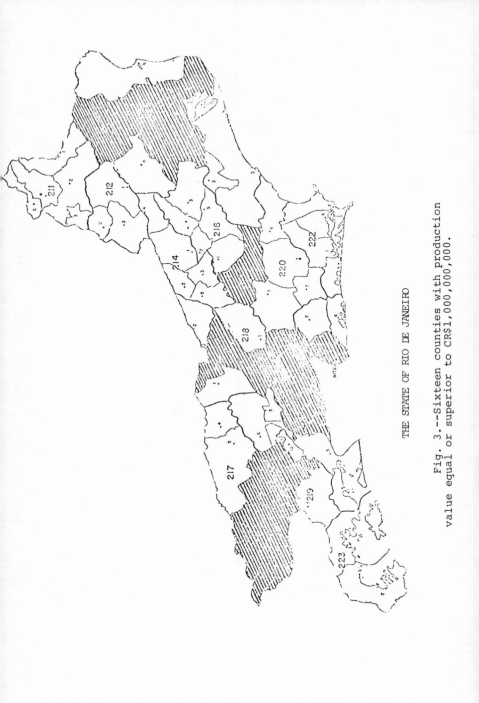

THE STATE OF RIO DE JANEIRO

Fig. 3.—Sixteen counties with production
value equal or superior to CR$1,000,000,000.

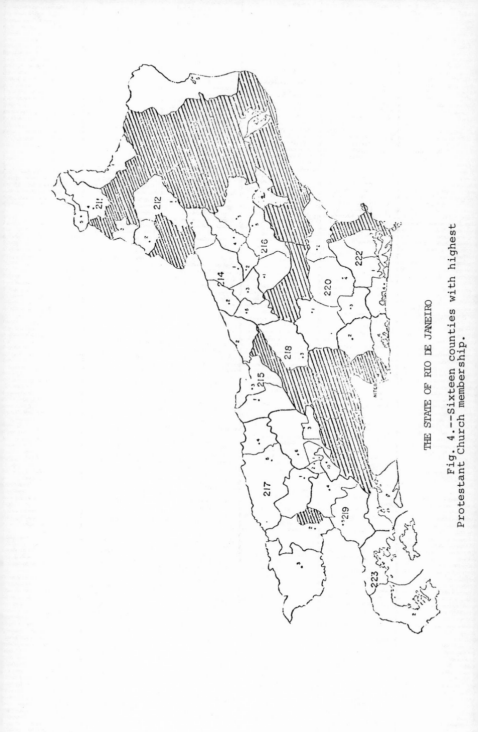

THE STATE OF RIO DE JANEIRO

Fig. 4.--Sixteen counties with highest
Protestant Church membership.

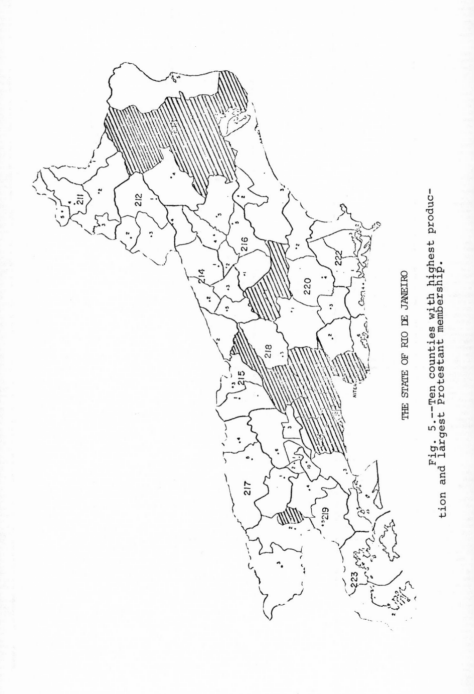

THE STATE OF RIO DE JANEIRO

Fig. 5.—Ten counties with highest production and largest Protestant membership.

In this microregion of the state where industry and population have come together, there is a high correlation between the scale of production value and Protestant church membership. It is clear, also, that the rate of growth in the industrialized Micro-Region 221 is found among the Pentecostal denominations.

Finding the Pentecostal growth particularly magnified in the urban industrialized area of Micro-Region 221 corresponds with the pattern discovered by William R. Read in his perceptive volume, *New Patterns of Church Growth in Brazil.* Mr. Read writes:

> The new pattern of church growth in Brazil has been accompanying, in a very remarkable way, the increase in the urban population that began in 1930--when this demographic trend is officially said to have begun. It is interesting to note that the Pentecostals did not begin their new pattern of church growth until after 1935, when urbanization began to accelerate. Pentecostal growth and urbanization seem to go together from 1935 to the present. This is the new significant fact we are witnessing in Brazil. Pentecostal Churches are found in the "high potential area" of Brazil. They can also be said to be the "high potential Churches" of the present missionary era. There is no indication that this "new pattern" of church growth is abating. On the contrary, it seems to be gaining momentum.[19]

Read is not alone in this discovery of accelerated Pentecostal growth in urban areas of culture change. Willems states in his significant study:

> What appears to be more relevant in the present context, however, is the fact that *growth on a large scale began only after 1930,* when the rate of social change picked up momentum and the traditional culture began to crack under the strain of the great depression, industrialization, and population increase.
>
> The assumption of a functional relationship between sociocultural change and the growth of Protestantism seems even more viable with regard to the development of the Pentecostal sects.[20]

Industrialization in Brazil has helped provide the climate and stage for sociocultural change which reaches to the masses of nearly 90,000,000 Brazilians. Industrialization is instrumental in providing the pull that draws the rural population from the subsistence level of life styles to the urban arena of sociocultural change and the better life.

NOTES

[1] Fernando de Azevedo, *Brazilian Culture*, Trans. by William Rex Crawford (New York: The MacMillan Co., 1950), p. 64.

[2] *Ibid.*, p. 63.

[3] *Ibid.*

[4] Werner Baer, "Socio-Economic Imbalances in Brazil," *New Perspectives of Brazil*, ed. Eric N. Baklano f (Nashville: Vanderbilt University Press, 1966), p. 138.

[5] Wagley, *op. cit.*, p. 76.

[6] Henry H. Keith and S. F. Edwards, eds., *Conflict and Continuity*, "Conflict and Continuity," by Jordon M. Young (Columbia: University of South Carolina Press, 1969), p. 257.

[7] Wagley, *op. cit.*, pp. 31-32.

[8] Baer, *op. cit.*, pp. 140-141.

[9] Lewis H. Young, ed., "Booming Brazil Finds a Key to Growth," *Business Week* (March 13, 1971), p. 90.

[10] Embassy of Brazil, "Centro Industrial de Aratu," *Boletim Especial*, No. 74 (April, 1971), p. 1.

[11] Murilo Melo Filho, "Brazil of the Seventies," *Manchete* (Rio de Janeiro, 1971), p. 33.

[12] *Ibid.*, p. 32.

[13] Joseph A. Kahl, *The Measurement of Modernism* (Austin: University of Texas Press, 1970), p. 3.

[14] IBGE, Serviço Nacional de Recensamento, *Atlas Censitário Industrial* (Rio de Janeiro: IBGE, 1965). The objective of the atlas is to focalize the geographic distribution of Brazilian industry according to the production value of 1959. Nine hundred and sixty-six of the counties of the nation's total of 2,778 are presented in the atlas. Only counties with production value superior to Cr$50,000,000 are presented.

[15] The official rate of exchange at this time was approximately Cr$200,000 to US$1.00.

[16]Additional information relative to the project is available in the "Brief Explanation of the Brazil Church Growth Computer Project" in the MARC department of World Vision International. The MARC/MIB Brazil project is directed by William R. Read in cooperation with Frank A. Ineson. Additional biographical information is found in Chapter 6. The author is grateful to these men for permitting the use of the Brazil Project material.

[17]IBGE, *Divisão do Brasil em Micro-Regiões Homogeneas 1968* (Rio de Janeiro: Instituto Brasileiro de Estatística, 1970), p. 352.

[18]IBGE, *Anuário Estatístico do Brasil 1968*, Vol. 29 (Rio de Janeiro: Fundação IBGE-Instituto Brasileiro de Estatística, 1968), p. 487.

[19]Read, *op. cit.*, p. 221.

[20]Willems, *op. cit.*, pp. 64-65.

Chapter 5

Decisions of Destiny – An Illustration

Life's destiny sometimes hinges upon a single decision or at
times upon a series of decisions. An illustration of this
can be found in the experiences of many Brazilians who made
their decision to leave the farm and family and make their
way to the cities. Some of these people are personal
acquaintances of the author.

These friends live in the industrial areas of Rio de
Janeiro, the Valley of the Paraiba River, and São Paulo.
They were requested to assist as respondents with this part
of the study of the catalytic effects of industrialization
on Protestant church growth in Brazil. Each of the respondents received five questionnaires to be completed by individuals who were active members of a Protestant church. The
questionnaire was composed of twenty-eight questions or
items. It was divided into four divisions. The first section of the questionnaire served to reveal the religious
history of the informant. The second division of the questionnaire served to illustrate the pattern of migration from
the rural to the urban areas. The third section projected
the industrial employment following the migration of the
informant to the new area. The fourth division was structured to provide an illustration of the participation of the
Protestants in promoting church growth in an industrialized
area.

A translation of the questionnaire will serve to clarify
its analysis which follows.[1]

QUESTIONNAIRE

We are making a study of the effects of industrialization on
the growth of the Protestant church in Brazil. Would you
please do us the favor of answering these questions in the
blanks provided.

I: <u>SPIRITUAL HISTORY</u>

1.   Name _____

2.   Date when became a member of the Protestant
     Church _____ Which church? _____

3.   Your age when you accepted Christ as your Saviour
     _____

4.   The city where you were converted _____

5.   Did your family always participate in the reli-
     gious festivals of your parish? Yes ___ No ___
     Sometimes ___

6.   Which festivals? _____

7.   How did you receive your first invitation to
     attend a Protestant church? Through:

     (1) fellow worker _____

     (2) neighbor   _____

     (3) stranger   _____

     (4) tract   _____

     (5) advertising   _____

     (6) radio   _____

     (7) other   _____

8.   Did you attend your first service in a home? ____
     or in a church building? ____ Which? ____

9.   Do you feel that your life became richer and hap-
     pier after becoming a member of a Protestant
     church?

     Yes _____ No _____ Not certain _____

II. <u>CHANGE OF RESIDENCE--MIGRATION</u>

10. The population of your home community was:

     (1)   0 - 300 persons   _____

(2) 300 - 500 persons _____

(3) 500 - 1000 persons _____

(4) 1000 - 5000 persons _____

(5) 5000 - indicate number _____

11. The reason for leaving the home community:

(1) Limited work opportunities _____

(2) Limited study opportunities _____

(3) Influenced to migrate to the industrial city by a friend or relative _____

(4) Opportunity for a better way of life for me and my family _____

(5) Other reason (please indicate) _____

12. Left the home community by railroad _____
bus _____ truck _____ other _____

13. Surface of roadway when departed from home community was dirt _____ stone _____ concrete _____ asphalt _____

14. Type of house in home community:
wooden _____ brick _____ other _____

15. Approximate distance from home community to industrialized city was _____ kilometers.

16. Type of house first used upon arrival in city:
frame _____ brick _____ other _____

17. How long did you live in your first residence before changing your residence?

(1) 6 months _____

(2) 1 year _____

(3) 2 years _____

(4) other _____ (please indicate)

18. What was your age when you left the home community to migrate to the industrial city? _____

III. INDUSTRIAL EMPLOYMENT

19. What type of work was available upon arrival in the city?

(1) factory _____

(2) gardening _____

(3) selling _____

(4) city government _____

(5) other _____ (please indicate)

20. How soon was industrial employment secured?

(1) 6 months _____

(2) other _____ (please indicate)

21. What type of article was being manufactured in the industry in which you first found employment?

automobile _____ paint _____ other _____

22. Do you feel the industrial city has provided you a better life economically than the home community would have offered you and your children?

Yes _____ No _____ Not certain _____

IV. CHURCH GROWTH

23. Is your church growing? Yes ___ No ___ Not certain ___

24. From your experience, do you find it is easier to invite neighbors who have recently moved into the industrial city to your church and promote their conversion, or to invite neighbors who have always lived in the industrial city?

_____

25. How many Pentecostals do you know at your place of work? _____

26. How many Presbyterians, Methodists, and/or Baptists do you know at your place of work? _____

27. Do you believe that as a Protestant with your convictions as to the necessity of honesty and serious work that you will have additional means to support your local church and its program of evangelization as time passes?

    Yes _____   No _____   Not sure _____

28. How many of your church members work in a factory?

    (1)   1 - 25%   _____

    (2) 25 - 50%   _____

    (3) 50 - 75%   _____

    (4) over 75%   _____

Item No. 1.--The name of the informant was requested for possible future identification. It was also requested in order to serve as a motivating force for careful completion of the questionnaire.

Item No. 2.--The date when the informant became a member of a Protestant church was requested. This revealed that one informant had been a member for more than thirty years. His date of membership was 1934. Another became a member of the Protestant church in the decade of the forties. Three became members of the Protestant church in the decade of the fifties; one in 1951, one in 1953, and one in 1957. Ten informants became members in the decade of the sixties. Five of these became members in 1968. Only one of the group became a member in the present decade. His date is 1971. Two of the informants did not respond to this item. It is illustrative from these responses regarding the date of church membership, that two-thirds of the number united with a Protestant church in the decade of the sixties. This illustrates the correlation between increasing industrialization and Protestant church growth.

Item No. 3.--The denominational membership of the informants is asked for in this third item. Ten denominations or sects were represented. They were: Presbiteriana (Presbyterian), Metodista (Methodist), Igreja do Nazareno (Church of the Nazarene), Evangélico Quadrangular (Four Square), Exército da Salvação (Salvation Army), Assembléia de Deus (Assembly of God), Nova Vida (New Life), Batista Bíblico (Bible Baptist), Presbiteriana Pentecostal (Pentecostal Presbyterian), Última Trombeta (Final Trumpet). This

list is evenly divided between the historic denominations
and pentecostal sects. The number of pentecostal informants
did not reach fifty per cent. This can be explained by the
fact that the respondents were not members of a pentecostal
denomination. The total number of Pentecostal Protestants
in Brazil now reaches to almost seventy per cent of the
Protestant membership in Brazil.

Item No. 4.--This item reveals the city or state where
the informant accepted the Protestant faith. Thirteen
cities including Sobradinho, a satellite city of the Federal
District, were represented. Four states: Sergipe, Minas
Gerais, São Paulo, and Rio de Janeiro were included. Two-
thirds were converted in the São Paulo-Rio area. This
illustrates the correlation between industrialized areas and
Protestant church growth.

Items Nos. 5 and 6.--These items concerned the participation of the informant's family in the religious festivals of
his parish. Two-thirds reported that there was no participation on the part of their family. Those who stated that
there was participation indicated that the Christmas season
was the time of most active participation. This pattern of
non-participation would seem to indicate its being a factor
in Protestant church growth.

Items Nos. 7 and 8.--These items regard the initial
contact with the Protestant Church on the part of the informant. Six types of contacts were suggested. Two-thirds of
the informants were first contacted by word of mouth. The
media of radio contact was second in order. This illustrates one of the most powerful factors responsible for the
rapid Protestant Church growth in industrialized areas. It
illustrated the pattern of contacting future members through
normal interpersonal relationships. This points to the
freedom experienced by the newly arrived into industrial
areas to freely experiment with new social contacts without
fear of family censure. This freedom to experiment, due in
part to the anomie which prevails in the industrial areas,
is another factor in the growth of the Protestant Church.
This illustration of initial contacts with the Protestant
Church through normal interpersonal relationships is an
important factor in the growth rate of the Protestant church
in Brazil. It is true that the newly arrived migrant to
impersonal urban areas senses feelings of acute loneliness
and displacement which would motivate him to find new and
warm relationships. However, the pattern of the Protestants, and particularly the Pentecostal sects, of contacting
the newly arrived is a primary motivation for seeking out
the social relationship offered in the Protestant church.
It is a "pull" factor operating within the Protestant
denominations.

Item No. 8.--Indicates the importance of the Protestant
cult within a church building. Two-thirds of the informants
contacted the Protestant "Culto" (worship) in a church

building of some type. These buildings could be large
churches seating 2,000 worshipers or small buildings. However, nearly a third made their initial visit to a Protestant worship conducted in a residence. This is illustrative
of the changing social conditions accompanying industrialization. There is a willingness to relate more freely with
strangers, or at least with others who are not a part of the
family kinship. This is particularly a characteristic of
the Protestants as they contact new people in the urban area
through their work and neighborhood relationships.

   Item No. 9.--This item had a 100% favorable response.
The informants experienced a fuller and more enjoyable life
in their new relationship as members of the Protestant
church. This would indicate that the Protestant church is
offering a social relationship that is satisfying to the
individual in transition from rural to urban life styles and
values. The Protestant values of sobriety, morality, industry, and thrift that were recognized by Weber as normative
for the Protestant denominations have been insisted upon by
most of the denominations for their members. Members in
such groups as the Assembléia de Deus (Assembly of God)
whose membership roll reaches nearly one million are provided with an identification card. If a member is not
issued a new card for reasons of deviations from the established norms and standards of the church, he is not per-
mitted to take part in the Communion service. This is
normally held during the afternoon of the first Sunday of
every month. According to the statistics of the *Culto Protestante*, there were 334,158 new Protestant church members in
all denominations admitted during the year 1968. There were
212,161 members excluded during the year.[2] This was a net
gain of 121,997. The major number of exclusions were from
the Pentecostal sects. The greatest number of new members
were received into the Pentecostal churches.

   Item No. 10.--Two-thirds of the informants migrated from
small cities of 5,000 to 11,000 to the industrialized areas
of metropolitan areas of São Paulo, Rio de Janeiro, and the
Valley of the Paraiba River. Migrants from the rural to the
urban areas are, as a rule, not equipped to work in industry. They are generally found in the third class of employment which is that of the services. These migrants in the
third level of employment work as carriers in the markets,
sweepers for the city, gardeners, and the women as domestic
servants. They do not have the educational and technical
qualifications to meet the requirements for factory
employment simply by migrating to the cities.

   Item No. 11.--This item is structured for the purpose of
identifying the reasons an individual leaves his home community to migrate to an industrialized area. One-third of
the informants left their home communities because of limited work opportunities. One-third hoped that the city
would offer a better life for them and for their family.
The others had various reasons which included "an opportun-

ity to participate in soccer," and "a desire to become
acquainted with great commercial centers." Still others
found that the city offered opportunities to study that were
limited in their city of origin. This is an illustration of
the "pull" factor of the city for increased economic,
social, and educational advantages. From these displaced
persons in the industrial milieu, the Protestant church
finds what Willems terms a "breeding ground par excellence
of religious dissent."[3]

Items Nos. 12 and 13.--These two items were placed in the
questionnaire to determine something of the transportation
problems that the migrant must solve in his move from the
rural to the urban. It was to be expected that not one made
the move by automobile, yet it was interesting to note this.
The migrants were nearly equally divided among the available
means of railroad, bus, and truck. The truck has been a
standard means of transporting migrants from one section of
Brazil to another. It is known as traveling by "pau de
arara," (the parrot roost). As many as fifty or more
migrants band together to hire a truck to transport them
from the northeast to the southern states where job opportunities seem greater and the dream for a better life holds
promise of fulfillment.

One of the migrants arrived at his destination by ship.
This possibility was open to those from the northeast who
did not find the overland travel on dirt roads to be an
attractive option. Overland travel from Recife to São
Paulo, before the construction of the present modern asphalt
road, was known to take as much as a month of travel time.
During the rainy season the trip could extend to almost two
months. This information was supplied to the writer by a
Minas Gerais state highway patrolman who had migrated to the
south of Brazil approximately fifteen years previously.
These roads were completed only during the last half of the
decade of the sixties. Two-thirds of the informants
reported that they had traveled on dirt roads from their
home communities to their present place of residence in the
industrialized areas. Only one had traveled over a concrete
highway. The four hundred kilometer Via Dutra connecting
the cities of Rio de Janeiro and São Paulo served for many
years as the most extensive continuous concrete highway in
the nation. Migrants from the smaller communities along the
highway would obviously use this concrete highway in moving
from the rural to the primate cities of Brazil or to the
regions of industrialization along the Valley of the Paraiba
River.

Item No. 15.--The informants traveled distances from as
near as 40 kilometers, to 2,500 kilometers to arrive at the
location where they expected to find conditions favorable
for a new life. These distances over poor highways systems
contributed to the breaking up of the traditional culture
and family relationships which were necessary before the
migrant would find within himself an openness to new relationships such as the Protestant church.

Items Nos. 14, 15, and 16.--These seem to indicate that
these informants, different from thousands, were not forced
by economic factors to find their first residence in the
favela areas surrounding the cities. This would be particularly true of Rio de Janeiro and São Paulo. The informants
all left brick housing to move to similarly constructed
houses. Only two moved from mud houses to brick, one moved
from a wooden house to a brick house. The *favelas* are
usually considered as slum areas. The poor conditions give
clear indications of a slum. However, it has been pointed
out by Professor Anthony Leeds that the *favelas* are not
characterized by deterioration of an area of the city. They
are rather areas that are in the process of development.
For example, electric lighting for the *favela* residents or a
water line to the *favela* are among some of the first marks
of a developing area rather than a slum.[4] Schools and
clinics are often built near the *favelas*.

Item No. 17.--This item adds to the illustration of relatively better economic conditions of our informants since
only one-fourth moved from their first residence in the new
area within a one-year period. Most remained for an
extended period. One remained for twenty years. This is an
obvious exception.

Item No. 18.--This item indicates that the migration from
the rural to the industrial area was a decision made by the
informant in his early adult years. This corresponds with
the reasons for seeking the industrialized region.

The third division of the questionnaire presented information regarding employment obtained in the new industrial
areas by the informants.

Item No. 19.--This item revealed that only one-third
found employment in the factories as their first place of
employment. This seems to illustrate the pattern of industrial areas pulling people but not necessarily for factory
employment, but rather for the level of services.

Item No. 20.--This item was structured to determine the
relative ease in obtaining employment in the new area. Such
responses as "immediately," "one day," "eight days," "fifteen days," or "one month," illustrates a new pattern emerging in the industrial area of relative ease in finding
employment. This is quite the opposite of the traditional
society and culture.

Item No. 21.--It was here revealed that the factory
employees among our informants were not employed in heavy
industry such as automobile production, but rather in light
industries. Light industries that were producing such consumer goods as foodstuffs, shoes, and clothing were indicated as the forms of first employment.

Item No. 22.--This item revealed that two-thirds of the informants believed that the city offers a better economic standard than the area from which they came. Only one had no opinion regarding the advantages or disadvantages economically, offered in the industrial area as opposed to the home community.

The fourth division of the questionnaire relates the involvement of the informant to the growth of the Protestant church in the industrial area.

Item No. 23.--This item indicates that 100% of the informants were agreed that their particular church was increasing in its membership. This illustrates the correlation of industrialization to the growth of the Protestant church.

Item No. 24.--This item indicated that all informants were actively participating in the program of church growth by contacting unchurched people. There was approximately an equal distribution of those who found that contacting newly arrived people was easier than contacting their neighbors to visit their churches. Approximately fifty per cent of the informants responded they found no difference in the relative ease of contacting the newly arrived or the long-time resident of the city for church attendance. This is illustrative of the activity among the Protestants to make it easier for migrants to find a new pattern of life, independent of the structures of the kinship ties and traditional loyalties.

Items Nos. 25 and 26.--These items were structured to reveal a possible pattern indicating the denominational loyalties of fellow workers of the informants. It would be expected that there would be a larger number of the Pentecostal membership represented. The informants, however, indicated that there was approximately an even distribution of Protestants between the historic and the Pentecostal denominations among their acquaintances at their place of employment. This does indicate that religion is an important topic of conversation.

Item No. 27.--This item regards the Protestant informant's ability to financially assist in the growth of his church. The consensus of opinion was that enlarged opportunity to aid the church would be derived from values held of the need for honesty and serious work patterns. This is illustrative of the effect economically of industrialization on Protestant church growth.

Item No. 28.--This item concludes the questionnaire by asking how many of the informant's fellow church members were employed in industry. One-fourth reported that from fifty to seventy-five per cent were employed in factories. One-fourth reported that from twenty-five to fifty per cent were employed in factories. This illustrates that probably not more than fifty per cent of the Protestant church

members of these churches were in the second level of
employment. It is reasonable to hold that the remainder of
the church members are employed in the third level of the
services.

The above questionnaire and its accompanying analysis is
presented as an illustration of the catalytic effect of
industrialization on Protestant church growth in the southern area of the industrial triangle linking Rio de Janeiro
and São Paulo with Belo Horizonte. The effect of stimulation is prominent. Industry asserts a pull that attracts
migrants to an opportunity area for social and economic
advancement in living standards. This in turn, effects the
environment stimulating an openness to Protestantism.

NOTES

[1] A copy of the Portuguese language questionnaire will be
found in the Appendix.

[2] Anuario Estatistico do Brazil, *op. cit.*, p. 487.

[3] Willems, *op. cit.*, p. 80.

[4] Class lecture at UCLA, May 5, 1971, Dr. Anthony Leeds,
"Urbanization in Brazil."

Chapter 6

Church Growth Experts Examine Brazil

Conversing with experts is exhilarating. No three men any-
where in the world have more knowledge about church growth
in general and church growth in Brazil in particular than
the three authorities who granted me the following interviews. Dr. Donald A. McGavran, William R. Read, and Frank A
Ineson are the three who are authorities on World, Latin
American, and Brazilian church growth: Each of these men
was gracious in granting interviews which were taped and
transcribed. Unfortunately, the interview of Dr. McGavran
was not adequately recorded. This was recognized immediately and his responses were written before leaving the
Church Growth Institute. Dr. Donald A. McGavran is director
of the Institute which is affiliated with the Fuller Theological Seminary located in Pasadena, California. He is the
author of several works on church growth.[1]

William R. Read initiated his service as a missionary to
Brazil in 1952. He has completed approximately twenty years
as a missionary of the United Presbyterian Church.

Mr. Read's first volume, *New Patterns of Church Growth in
Brazil*, is a significant study of the accelerated Protestant
church growth in Brazil. It has been translated into the
Portuguese under the title *Fermento Entre As Masses (Ferment
Among the Masses)*.[2] Mr. Read is at present serving as Technical Director of the Brazil research computer project co-
sponsored by MARC/MIB (Missions Advanced Research and Communications Center and Missionary Information Bureau of Brazil). The project utilizes the facilities and technical
assistance of World Vision International.

Mr. Frank A. Ineson served twenty years as an economist
in the Forstry Department of the United States Government.
For the past six years Mr. Ineson has served as Executive
Secretary of the Missionary Information Bureau of Brazil.
Mr. Ineson stated in his interview that "there are over 150
missionary agencies in Brazil and over 100 of them cooperate
with MIB. There are nearly 3,000 missionaries in Brazil and
around 2300 of them subscribe for MIB services." Mr. Ineson
is cooperating in the MARC/MIB Brazil project.

It was this writer's conviction that these three men, if they would agree to share their knowledge, could materially contribute to this study of the effect of industrialization on the growth of the Protestant church in Brazil.

A series of questions were prepared and an interview was granted by each of the authorities. [3]

It is my purpose to present the questions and responses within a united structure. This method will contribute to an understanding of the consensus or divergence of thought among the three authorities on Latin American culture and Protestant church growth. This in turn is helpful in the analysis of the items individually and the three interviews as a composite whole. Some meaningful relationships between industrialization and Protestant church growth can in this way be discovered.

Item No. 1.--In what ways do you find that industrialization in Latin America is affecting its culture? In what way or ways do you find that Brazil has been affected by industrialization?

Dr. McGavran: "In every way, it is fast becoming a part of the one-world culture that is rapidly forming." [4]

An example cited by Dr. McGavran was the use of common building materials such as reinforced concrete for building in Buenos Aires or in Los Angeles. The use of electricity is also an example.

Mr. Read: "It is a process the sociologists call modernization . . . Industrialization is part and parcel of this whole process, and this is affecting its culture in a very radical way." [5]

Modernization and industrialization are part of a pattern of change in the traditional Latin American society. The traditional rural pattern is breaking up and there is a flight to the cities through internal migration. It is a new settlement pattern changing from the rural to the urban. The countries of Latin America have always had a primate city. Brazil has two primate cities: Rio de Janeiro and São Paulo. These are islands of modernization.

Industrialization is affecting Brazil's culture by establishing a whole new life style for the people who are entering the cities. Mr. Read clearly defined the area of greatest social and cultural change in Brazil when he stated:

In Brazil you find an area that is very well defined as far as its industrial activity. . . . The industrial zone of Sao Paulo is being connected with that of Rio de Janeiro by the valley of the Paraiba River. Its industrialization began in the 40's with the steel mills of Volta Redonda. Then you go a little to the North of Rio

to Juiz de Fora which has always been the center of the
textile industry in Brazil and then on to the north to
Belo Horizonte. There you get into the whole area of
iron ore. If you connect these three cities . . . this
is the outstanding industrial zone in Latin America. So
I say the changes are occurring in this particular zone
and you have a middle class emerging in this particular
area, perhaps faster than in any other part of Latin
America.[6]

I lived and worked four years in the Belo Horizonte side
of this triangle. Industrialization was progressing rapidly
in the four years preceding the Revolution of March 31,
1964. My personal experience motivated an extra question at
this juncture of the interview. I questioned Mr. Read
regarding his knowledge as to the beginnings of this particular surge of industrialization. His reply was in the form
of a brief history of the introduction of coffee into Brazil
and its consequences including the building of the railroads
in the São Paulo stimulated the increase of wealth. This
wealth was then transferred into industrialization means for
the development of the country. This source of capital had
its beginnings in the 1850's and by approximately 1890 the
railroads were built.

Mr. Read next spoke of the new industrialization to be
found in Brazil. He classified it as a problem facing Brazil's industrialization. There must be a recognition of
present-day capital intensive as opposed to the intensive of
labor in the past. In the past a new factory would employ
large numbers of people. This is an example of labor intensive. With the appearance of capital intensive, industry
does not employ great numbers of people but rather purchases
modern automated machinery. Mr. Read employed an illustration of the new industrialization with its concurrent problem of underemployment for the nation. A new synthetic
rubber plant was constructed in Recife. The factory covered
a ground space of forty acres. But, it only required forty
people to maintain its operation. The factory only required
a limited number of personnel to control the temperature and
to operate the control panel. A small crew was needed for
the work of maintaining the stock of raw material coming
into the factory. Another small crew was employed to handle
the finished products.

Mr. Read continued:

One would think that industrialization is going to solve
the problem of Brazil. It's not. Because you don't have
the people employed as before. . . . The assembly line in
automotive is modernized. Ford ten years ago brought
their old machines down, but now they are in the stage of
bringing their new machines down. And so now instead of
having fifteen employed on a hundred foot of assembly
line, the new assembly line will take only two.[7]

This would then tend toward unemployment in an over-populated city. "So, the industrialization in Brazil is not going to be cure-all for the development of the country."[8]

However, industrialization has affected the growth of the Protestant church in Brazil. The churches, particularly the large Pentecostal ones, are providing a warm community for the reception of the rural migrants. The new relationships experienced in the community of the church replaces the loyalties of the rural community. The church members become the family of the newly arrived individuals. The churches "catch them at a time in their lives when they are most receptive for new ideas and these people are accepting what we call the Gospel."[9]

Through a radical transition in their lives, which is termed conversion, the rural migrants experience a feeling of community and belonging. Baptism and church membership are then experienced. New patterns and life styles are accepted as members of the migrant family become involved in the church. The wife and mother becomes involved in the women's group. The children take part in the activities of their age group. The husband and father finds comradeship with the men's group of the church.

Industrialization is a pull factor drawing the flow of migrants to the urban areas of Brazil. The Protestant churches in the area which respond to the influx of migrants experience rapid growth.

Mr. Ineson: There are two aspects of industrialization in Brazil. It involves the location and size of factories. Major factories have been established in São Paulo. On the other hand, there has been an establishment of small factories all over Brazil. These are found primarily in the North and Northeast regions. They are small satellite industries that produce parts for the large industries in the São Paulo area. There is a decentralization as well as a centralization of industry in Brazil.

These satellite industries perform the same function in Brazil as they perform in the United States. In the measure that the modern automated factories employ fewer and fewer people, the satellite industries are employing a greater number of people. This more than compensates for the modernization. "Modernization in Brazil up to this point, and the expansion of the economy has been such that it is more than absorbing the people."[10] Industrialization has motivated the movements of people. The pattern has been from the rural to the urban. Mr. Ineson made the observation that his surveys indicate that Protestants move more readily than Catholics."[11] He commented further that his "observation is that industrialization in Brazil has resulted in lifting the social status of the people generally."[12]

Item No. 2.--Do you find that rapid Protestant church growth is always or nearly always related to the phenomenon of industrialization? Is it valid to expect rapid church growth in Latin America in areas of expanding industrial activity?

Dr. McGavran: "No. However, there is a possibility for church growth in industrial areas."[13]

It is valid to expect rapid church growth where there is sufficient work being carried on. Church growth is not something automatic. An industrial area could have ten churches and one of them would grow. The reason is that more work and activity would be carried on by that church.

Dr. McGavran illustrated this principle of cause and effect by suggesting that if ten men go out to fish for trout, they will not all come home with a creel full of fish. It will be the man who has walked the farthest on the rocks of the stream who will come back with the most fish. It will not be the man who has only gone one hundred yards.

Mr. Read: "Rapid church growth can be expected if there is a church or if there are churches who have mobilized their lay people to evangelize. Churches that are mobilized in the urban areas will register rapid growth.

Other areas where rapid or outstanding Protestant church growth could be expected are in frontier areas. The people who migrate to these lands are already three to six per cent of the Protestant church.

Rapid church growth, according to Mr. Read, seems to be related to the phenomenon of industrialization.

Mr. Ineson: Rapid church growth can be expected in the traditional churches as a result of industrialization. This is a normal pattern among these churches as a result of migration. There is question, however, if this rapid growth is a result of additions due to conversions. Mr. Ineson has discovered that industrialization usually results in increased materialistic interests among the industrial workers. He has not found empirical evidence of correlation between industrialization and conversions among those people who are taking their primary role in the industrialization process.

Rapid church growth can be expected among the Pentecostal sects as a result of industrialization. The growth of these churches is primarily among the masses who have been attracted to the industrial urban areas by the hope of better economic conditions than those where they formerly lived on a subsistence level. The Northeast is such an area. Most rural areas are of the subsistence level.

The Pentecostal churches in the industrial areas grow as a result of additions by conversion. However, this is a different facet of church growth since the growth is among the lower classes, and not among the industrial classes. Mr. Ineson sees the increased Protestant growth among the Pentecostals as a result of displaced people harassed by low economic conditions persisting in the industrial area. In addition to the low economic conditions, they experience insecurity, trouble, and a searching after solutions for their problems.

Item No. 3.--Do you believe that there will be increasingly accelerated church growth in Brazil as the traditional areas, e.g., the Northeast, become modernized and industrialized?

Dr. McGavran: There is opportunity for accelerated growth in the traditional areas that are becoming modernized and industrialized. There is nothing that precludes an effect of rapid church growth because of increase in industrialization in a traditional area. It is a fact that the anomie of the city and the loneliness of the people contribute to them being winnable.

Mr. Read: The process of modernization will occur as the people move to the industrialized areas.

Mr. Ineson: There is an excellent church growth rate in the Northeast. This can be attributed to the activity of the national church rather than to the foreign missionaries. The national church has taken over the burden of evangelism in the Northeast. Missionaries found the Northeast and especially the interior, a difficult place to live. Until very recently there were no good roads and the area was subject to periodic droughts and occasional floods.

The traditional churches and the Pentecostals have both had an excellent rate of growth in the Northeast. The Protestant growth rate has been double that of demographic rate. This means that there has been approximately a six per cent growth rate in the church.

The development of the Northeast has been stimulated by aids to industrialization. The people are hopeful. Cities in the Northeast are being electrified. Six years ago there were cities such as Forteleza which had no electricity except that provided by a generator. This was only for a period of two or three hours each day. Forteleza, as well as other cities in the Northeast, are now blooming with their newly installed electric systems. This type of modernization is changing the old life styles and opening to the people new ways of living.

Another aid toward industrialization and mobility is the highway system that is being rapidly opened from the Northeast leading into the Amazon basin. An existing highway to

the South has for approximately the entire decade of the
sixties been a factor in the opening of the Northeast to the
influence of the industrialized South.

Item No. 4.--Where could one expect the greatest Protestant church growth to be in Brazil during the next ten
years? Why do you foresee a rapid growth in these areas?

Dr. McGavran: Rapid growth among the Protestant churches
could probably be expected in the cities. Brazil is the
only country in the world where the churches are growing in
the large cities. Most other countries of the world do not
have urban church growth. The usual pattern is conversion
in the rural areas and then migration to the cities. An
example of this pattern can be found in the city of Bombay.
The city has a seven per cent Protestant population. There
is only a two per cent rural population. Those converted in
the rural area migrate to the city to increase the percentage of Protestants in Bombay. The church, however, is not
increasing through converts from the urban area. Portuguese
South America is an exception to the rule for there the
Protestant church growth is in the cities as well.

Mr. Read: "There are high potential areas for Protestant
church growth. These are opportunity areas and are found in
such places as the Pato Branco (White Duck) region of southern Paraná. The state of Paraná is a dynamic combination of
agriculture and industry. Much of this is still in the
pioneer stage. Pato Branco is pioneer in agricultural
development with some small industry. There is a network of
roads developing. A transportation system for distributing
consumers' products is a necessity. Agricultural products
also need to flow into the cities. This particular area is
just in the process of developing. It is only ten years old.
Industrialization is in the pioneer stage just as banking,
construction, education, and politics are all in the initial
stages. Tourism to the Iguaçu Falls is also rapidly expanding as a result of modern roads.

Church growth can be expected in areas such as this in
southern Paraná where there is an economic base forming.
The people in an area like this are in a receptive attitude
to innovation. The combination of frontier and industrial
activity is fertile territory for Protestant church growth
in Brazil.

I expressed surprise with the answer from Mr. Read that
indicated his expectancy of Protestant church growth in the
frontier-industrial regions rather than in the rapidly growing industrial metropolitan areas. Large Pentecostal church
buildings are under construction in São Paulo. I am
acquainted with the building that Manuel de Mello is con-
structing in São Paulo. The entrance to the building is
presently being used for worship services. It seats eight
thousand worshipers. The auditorium is planned for twenty-
five thousand.

Mr. Read sees Manuel de Mello as a charismatic leader of the masses and as unique in his position. Manuel de Mello is a champion of the people and finds his followers among the migrants who have entered the São Paulo area. Many of them are among the masses that are dwelling in the *favelas*. The large church which will seat twenty-five thousand and provide standing room for ten thousand more, is an expression of a shelter for the masses. He has the role of their *patrão* (employer or boss). They look to him for all the answers and of course he attempts to give them the answers for their religious questions.

Mr. Ineson: Mr. Ineson did not answer this question directly, but rather indicated the findings of some of his recent studies related to membership requirements and the activity of the various denominations in Brazil. Some of these discoveries suggest possible trends in Protestant church growth and by analysis would yield information regarding locations of future church growth. He suggested that many factors need to be considered before indicating exact locations where Protestant church growth could be expected. A heavy concentration of Baptists would be indicative of a location for future church growth. Mr. Ineson pointed out the result of his study relating to activity ratio showed that the Baptists were higher than the other traditional Protestant denominations. It was also significant that his findings indicate approximately the same ratio of high activity among Protestant denominations in the political, social, and economic levels of life.

Item No. 5.--Do you believe the traditional, e.g., historic, Protestant denominations in Brazil are evangelizing as effectively as possible among the migrants? For example, are they serving as effectively as possible among the migrants to the city of São Paulo.

Dr. McGavran: In reply to this question, Dr. McGavran responded with a definite "No!" He stated that these churches were middle class and proud of their status. It has taken them out of contact with the masses that are migrating to areas such as São Paulo more rapidly than they are moving into the city. Mr. Ineson noted that their conversion record is not outstanding in the city of São Paulo.

Item No. 6.--Is it reasonable to hold that the Pentecostal sects in Brazil are definitely encouraged in their growth by the developing of a great industrial park?

Dr. McGavran: Another "No" was the response to this question by Dr. McGavran. The great industrial park does not assure growth for the Protestant church, nor do the cities of today assure it.

Mr. Read: The pull factor of a great industrial park is very strong. There will be a great influx of people. The great masses that are pulled to the industrial park, how-

ever, will not benefit greatly through working in industry.
Where a great mass of people have been gathered into an
area, there will be accelerated activity among the Pentecostals who proclaim the Gospel in the language of the common
man and demand a verdict. The Pentecostal sects are definitely encouraged by the great industrial parks. The traditional churches are not there. They are not out where the
humble people are.

Mr. Ineson: It is not the development of a great industrial park that encourages the growth of the Pentecostal
sects, but the related effects associated with its development. The social level of the people who are being converted in the Pentecostal churches during the last ten to
twenty years is definitely moving upwards. The social level
is higher among Protestants than it is among the Brazilian
population as a whole. However, the Pentecostal sects are
not having large success among the middle classes of Brazil.

Item No. 7.--Could the historic denominations grow as
rapidly as the Pentecostal groups in Brazil without major
functional, structural modifications?

Dr. McGavran: They could not. However, they could
easily make the necessary changes in order to reach the
masses. Dr. McGavran did not suggest what changes needed to
be made other than a willingness to serve the masses. He
related a very interesting case in which a Presbyterian lay-
man in a city located one hundred miles west of Recife found
an abandoned Presbyterian church. It was located near a
favela. There were no positive responses given by leaders
of his church to reopen the church. The man went alone.
When Dr. McGavran visited the church there were four hundred
people from the *favela* actively involved in worship. All
was under the leadership of the people themselves.

Mr. Read: The historic churches are pastor-oriented and
the people are observers, not participators. There is a
phenomenon among the historic churches which is attempting
to change this structure. There are "renewal groups" breaking off from the denominations.

The Pentecostal sects are lay-oriented and lay-
structured. These groups are an important growing edge in
the rapid Protestant church growth in Brazil.

Major functional-structural modifications are necessary.

Mr. Ineson: Mr. Ineson believed that a question such as
this assumes something that would be hard to prove. He
believes that the Presbyterians should accept their opportunity of influencing the middle and upper classes of Brazil. It would be a case of not expecting rapid growth as is
experienced by the Pentecostals among the masses. They are

working with the eighty to eighty-five per cent of the population of Brazil. These are the people who are lacking
security economically and socially.

Item No. 8.--When could the present rate of rapid Protestant church growth in Brazil be expected to deaccelerate?

Dr. McGavran: This could be expected to happen when
there is a Marxist government takeover. However, Dr.
McGavran did not expect this to happen. He expressed himself as considering Marxism as a religion. The rate of
growth could be expected to deaccelerate if there were an
occurrence of radical Roman Catholic oppression. This again
was not expected by Dr. McGavran. His final statement concerned the possibility of the church turning to social
action and social concerns, and failing to proclaim the
Gospel. If any of these three occurred there would be a
deacceleration of the present rapid Protestant church growth.

Mr. Read: There is a fifty-fifty rural-urban balance at
the present in Brazil. Fifty per cent of the nation is
rural and fifty per cent is urban. The decade of the seventies will see a continued urbanization in Brazil. The
nation will become sixty per cent urban during the next ten
years. The existing pattern of rapid church growth will
continue through the present decade. Mr. Read believes that
by 1980 the question will be answered. The pastors of the
traditional churches will be in a position to answer this
question as to whether the rate of growth is to deaccelerate or continue after that time.

Some of the historic churches are in a period of deacceleration. The Episcopal church is declining. The Methodists
have reached a plateau.

There are some areas of Brazil where the migration of the
people to the industrialized regions has resulted in a loss
of people. These areas will deaccelerate.

Mr. Ineson: The indications, according to Mr. Ineson,
are that there has already begun a process of deacceleration.
An example of this is the group Brasil Para Cristo (Brazil
for Christ) of which Manuel de Mello is the leader. The
consensus is that it has been on the downgrade for the last
couple of years. However, there is a normal deacceleration
that is going to appear because the bases for measuring the
Protestant growth are getting larger and larger. This will
show a decrease in the rate of growth.

Item No. 9.--Do you believe that the pattern of rapid
church growth in the highly industrialized areas of Brazil
will eventually be reflected in other areas?

Dr. McGavran: There will be a reflection of the rapid
growth of the industrialized areas in other regions of Brazil through the movements of people. Migration of Protes-

tants who are pulled to new regions of Brazil for economic reasons will be responsible for this.

Mr. Read: Opportunity areas in Brazil such as the frontier-industrial regions will reflect the growth of the present industrialized areas. The region comprising the western part of the state of São Paulo, southern Mato Grosso, and Goiás state are going to receive a tremendous impetus toward modernization as a result of the hydroelectric plant of Urubupungá under construction on the Paraná River. The growth of the churches in the industrial areas will be reflected in this region. Another area where the growth of the church will be reflected is that area between the state of Espírito Santo and Belo Horizonte, the capital city of the state of Minas Gerais. All of the Paraiba Valley and the cities on the routes connecting the industrial triangle of São Paulo, Rio de Janeiro, and Belo Horizonte. There is another region surrounding the city of Porto Alegre that is growing rapidly. These nineteen counties will reflect the rapid Protestant church growth.

These high potential areas will be reached by a high potential church that is acceptable to the masses. These masses are receptive as a consequence of social innovations.

Mr. Ineson: Reflection of the present church growth into other areas will be a result of the migration of peoples. This is something that should be studied further; for church growth depends upon transfer growth as well as conversions. The growth of the church in a particular, and the rate with which it develops will depend upon the migration factor as well as the new accessions.

Item No. 10.--In what way or ways would you understand the pattern of secularization of the Western Industrial culture to affect the growth of the Protestant church in Brazil?

Dr. McGavran: The pattern of secularization will reach Brazil. It will become a secular society. This will not happen as rapidly as in North America, but it will come.

Mr. Read: Brazil is at the take off stage in its development. He feels that the structure of the labor foce will affect the pattern of church growth. The number of the economically active population that is Protestant will affect the growth of the Protestant church. Urbanization and the filling up of the cities will have an effect. For example, the ten largest cities in Brazil had a population in 1950 of eight million people. Today these same cities have a population of twenty-eight million. In 1980 these ten cities will have a population of approximately thirty-five million. The future of the nation lies in these cities.

There will be an increasing freedom of social mobility. The masses must be free to move up in the stratas of

society. Mr. Read believes that Protestantism reaches the
masses in the lower echelons of society and then they begin
to move upward.

Secularization will be a part of the developing social
milieu of Brazil. The measure that it affects the culture
of Brazil will not be the same as it has affected other
nations. It must pass through the Brazilian mind and
personality.

Item No. 11.--What kind of church growth can be expected
in an area of high mobility? Is there reason to believe
that a great influx of people can be expected in the church
if as many as four-fifths of those living in the area are
planning to move to another area?

Dr. McGavran: This question was directed to Dr. McGavran
as a result of a study of the high mobility of Brasília,
which is one of the major regions of migration in Brazil.
The Federal District is not an industrialized area. It has
been an area of pull for Brazilians from the northeast, particularly. It is a region of high mobility. Dr. McGavran
saw no reason for expecting rapid church growth. He did see
it as an opportunity for extending the church growth into
other regions where the pull for a better life was stronger.

Summary

A summary of the analysis of the interviews with
Dr. Donald A. McGavran, William R. Read, and Frank A. Ineson
yields seven generalizations regarding the relationship of
industrialization to Protestant church growth in Brazil.
They are as follows:

1. There is general agreement that industrialization in
Brazil is one segment of the whole process of modernization.
It was further indicated that Brazil is rapidly becoming a
part of the one-world culture. Industrialization is causing
a change in the social patterns and life styles of Brazil.
The traditional loyalties to the *patrão* and to the extended
family relationship are breaking up as the flow of migrants
continues from the rural to the industrial-urban areas.
Industrialization should not be considered as the panacea
for all the social and economic problems demanding an answer
in Brazil. However, industrialization has affected the
Protestant church growth by amassing great numbers of people
in one area who are open and receptive to its message and
community.

Rapid Protestant church growth should not be thought of
as an automatic effect of industrialization. Rapid church
growth can be expected as a result of migration into the
industrialized regions. This is a normal pattern in the
growth of the historic denominations. The Pentecostal sects
avail themselves of the opportunity presented in the indus-

trial area to interact with the newly arrived to the area
and are experiencing excellent growth.

2. Opportunity for accelerated Protestant church growth
can also be found in the traditional areas of Brazil. This
is true of areas such as the northeast in their transition
from the colonial and traditional culture to twentieth-
century modernization and industrialization.

3. Brazil presents high potential for church growth in
the large cities. This is an exception to the rule. The
general rule is that large cities are not receptive areas.
Another high potential area is to be found in the regions of
frontier-industrial development.

4. The rapid church growth experienced by the Pentecostal sects in the industrial centers of Brazil will not be
experienced by the traditional, historic denominations until
functional and structural changes are considered and imple-
mented which will aid these churches to interact with the
masses.

5. The pattern of accelerated Protestant church growth
should not normally deaccelerate during the decades of the
seventies. The flight to the cities as an effect of the
pull of modernization and industrialization will continue.
The Brazilian urban population will reach sixty per cent
before 1980.

6. Rapid Protestant church growth as found in the industrialized areas will be reflected in new areas of Brazil as
a result of migration of the Protestant population. The
activity of the Pentecostal churches in these high potential
regions will also affect the church growth.

                            NOTES

[1] The most recent volume of Dr. Donald A. McGavran is
Understanding Church Growth (Grand Rapids: William B.
Eerdmans, 1970).

[2] Mr. Read co-authored the volume *Latin American Church
Growth*, 1969. Victor M. Monterroso and Harmon A. Johnson
collaborated with Mr. Read.

[3] A list of the questions is included in the Appendix.
Dr. McGavran was also asked concerning mobility of migrants.

[4] Interview with Donald A. McGavran, May 5, 1971.

[5] Interview with William R. Read, May 5, 1971.

[6] *Ibid.*

[7] *Ibid.*

[8]*Ibid.*

[9]*Ibid.*

[10]Interview with Frank A. Ineson, May 5, 1971.

[11]*Ibid.*

[12]*Ibid.*

[13]McGavran, *op. cit.*

Chapter 7

Christian Opportunity in Modern Brazil

The rise of industrialization in Brazil is producing a new cultural pattern for the nation. There is a unity that is pulling Brazil together. The regionalism characteristic of North and South Brazil is weaving itself into a national unity. Innovations in the economic life of the nation are affecting it socially, politically, psychologically, recreationally, and religiously. Modern Brazil is rising.

Primary social relationships expressed in family living and kinship control are changing. There is an increasing emphasis upon the nuclear family in the rising industrial society and less upon the traditional extended family relationships. The paternalistic pattern of control and the importance of nepotism is losing its strength with the emergence of available means of economic independence. However, this is not to imply that the family relationships are not important in Brazil. It is only that there is change taking place in primary social relationships.

The city of São Paulo experiences an exodus of population on the weekends that rivals the Los Angeles exodus to the desert, to the mountains, and to Las Vegas. These "Paulistanos" traveling north are seeking the social benefits of family relationship in the interior. Granted, there is also an exodus south to the beaches of Santos and Guarujá for leisure and recreation. I have traveled into the city of São Paulo on Friday evenings and the divided highway, the Via Anangueira, has been one great congestion of modern traffic and blinding lights. My experience has been that traveling north to Campinas on Sunday night the traffic is the same until midnight and later. The Sao Paulo-bound "pista" is solid automobile traffic.

I would agree with Dr. McGavran who finds that there is a fast emergence in Brazil of the one-world culture. Mr. Read saw the effect of industrialization as being a radical change. I believe that this study has shown that the changes are of such a nature that they should be termed revolutionary. Mr. Ineson saw the great effect demonstrated in the migrations from the rural areas to the industrial-urban areas.

There is ferment in the masses of traditional Brazil. A middle class is emerging as a result of the social mobility provided through the economic effects of industrialization and increasing modernization.

It is in the cities that innovations are a pattern expected and accepted by the Brazilians. Richard Graham recognized the beginnings of social changes being initiated in Brazilian cities. Graham states:

> In Brazil cities were the beachheads of the modern world. Urban groups wished to approximate the models created in Europe in their economic organization, social structure, attitudes and style of life.[1]

The cities were the beachheads for cultural innovations for the Brazilians in the Imperial period of the nation's history. They are the scenes of action in the modern milieu.

The catalytic action of industrialization on Protestant church growth is centered in industrial cities. This is pointed out in the results of our study of the sixteen counties of the state of Rio de Janeiro with the highest industrial production and of the sixteen counties with the largest Protestant membership. These counties are the "municípios" or cities with the surrounding areas. Ten of these counties are in both classifications. The most significant finding was that the Micro-Region 221 included seven of the counties from each classification.

The results of these statistical findings closely parallel the findings of Emilio Willems in his study of the state of São Paulo with its twenty-three ecological zones. Willems found that the greatest concentration of Protestants was to be found in the Industrial Zone which includes the capital city of São Paulo and the surrounding satellite cities. The Industrial Zone accounted for 58.1 per cent of the Protestants of the state of São Paulo. It was from findings such as this that Willems was able to state:

> Our hypothesis of an historical concomitance between the expansion of Protestantism and the emergence of an industrialized and urbanized society was borne out by the facts.[2]

Micro-Region 221 has 43.68 per cent of the Protestant church membership of the state of Rio de Janeiro. This is one of the bases of our generalizations describing industrialization as directly affecting Protestant church growth. It was further shown that 84.1 per cent of the Protestants of the Micro-Region 221 reside in six counties of the Micro-Region which have a production value of over one billion cruzeiros each.

It is in these industrial cities where the outstanding church growth is registered. The large Pentecostal churches, particularly, are providing a warmth of community for the newly arrived migrants from the rural areas of the traditional patterns of Brazilian society.

Protestant church growth is not something automatic. This generalization is true even in areas of cultural innovations where industrialization is yielding a measurable influence. I agree with the following responses of the three men interviewed regarding the relation of rapid church growth in Brazil to increased industrialization.

The validity of expecting rapid church growth, according to Dr. McGavran, can only be based upon the exercise of sufficient work and activity on the part of the church which finds itself geographically situated to grow. The effective mobilization of a church's membership for evangelization, according to Read, is reason for expecting rapid church growth. Mr. Ineson expects automatic church growth in established traditional churches in areas of industrialization as a result of migration of church members pulled by industry to the areas. He also expects the migrant masses to rapidly fill the membership of the Pentecostal churches. They would be drawn into the membership through conversion. This is another way of expressing the necessity for activity on the part of the local church which is mobilized for evangelism and geographically situated in the environment of cultural change.

There are theological reasons for the growth of the Protestant church in Brazil, as well as for the growth of the universal Church of Jesus Christ, that are presupposed by these authorities. These theological reasons for the growth of the Church are grounded in the character and purpose of God in the world as revealed in the Scriptures in the Old and New Testaments.

God has a mission in the world today. He Himself controls this mission. The Almighty God is shaking the foundations of the twentieth-century world. People who lived under the old systems of government are faced today with democracy and communism, with a world civilization, with rising expectations for a better life, with scientific breakthroughs, and with the revelation of God in Christ. God desires to redeem all mankind. "It is not a man-initiated activity but *missio Dei*, who Himself remains in charge of it."[4]

Barriers of time and space are rapidly disappearing in the modern world. Jet transportation links continents while modern communication links nations in a fraction of a second. Peasants who migrate to urban areas are noticeably affected by the impact of the modern world. Likewise, the average modern sophisticated person from a developed nation has a visable reaction when he discovers the universality of

the modern civilization. It is in such a world that the
Protestant church in Brazil is rapidly gaining adherents
among those people who have been launched into the twentieth-century culture. It is in such a changing world that
the universal church acts redemptively.

The Protestant churches and sects in Brazil subscribe to
the theological position of a dynamic relationship to the
Church of Jesus Christ and therefore assume responsibility
in the mission of God in Brazil.

The traditional cultural areas of Brazil will yield to
the innovations of the new industrialized society and provide increasing opportunities for Protestant church growth.
There will come in the areas, such as the north-eastern section of Brazil, the breakup of the subsistence level of
socioeconomic life styles as the forces of modernization,
urbanization, and industrialization push into the area. Dr.
McGavran emphasized the opportunity for growth as the
process of modernization and industrialization continue.
Mr. Ineson revealed his opinion that the Protestant church
was already growing rapidly in northeast Brazil as a result
of the activity of the Brazilian church. His findings
coupled with the opportunity for expected rapid church
growth would lead one to generalize that some of the greatest opportunities for increased Protestant membership could
be expected in the northeast.

Protestant church growth indicates a larger number of
people who are changing in their life styles from the traditional patterns. They are in the process of accepting the
Protestant values of industry, morality, economy, and the
working in a vocation for the glory of God. They do make
good workers for industry. As industry develops in the
northeast of Brazil there will be an increasing number of
people who will be ready to take advantage of the opportunity industrialization offers for attaining the goal of a
better life.

There are high potential areas for Protestant church
growth developing in Brazil as a result of industrialization
and modernization. Again it is the cities of Brazil where
the growth rate of the Protestant church should be expected.
Dr. McGavran indicated the cities as areas of growth in his
answer to the question concerning areas of expected church
growth during the next ten years. The percentage of urban
dwellers will reach sixty per cent by 1980. This would be
an estimated population of sixty-five to seventy million
people in the Brazilian cities. Ten of the largest cities
will have an estimated population of between thirty and
thirty-five million people. Another area of expected Protestant church growth would be in the frontier-industrial
areas. This was pointed out by Mr. Read. There are
variables that determine the growth of the church in these
areas. The expected growth in the urban areas would not
occur if the large Pentecostal churches did not continue to

express interest in the newly arrived migrants attracted to the cities by the pull of industry. The historic churches must increase their activity. Similarly, the frontier-industrial areas would not experience expanded growth if the Protestants would fail to migrate to these particular areas of opportunity to serve as the innovators of religious change.

The historic denominations in Brazil have tended to move up and away from the social level of the masses. Mobility up in society is a characteristic of the Protestant sects and churches. There is a transition that occurs that renders the denomination ineffective in reaching the people of the lower classes. Liston Pope has carefully indicated this by stating:

A sect, as it gains adherents and the promise of success, begins to reach out toward greater influence in society, whatever the roots of its ambition may be--evangelistic fervor, denominational rivalry, ministerial desire for greater income and influence, the cultural vindication of its peculiar faith, or what not. In the process it accommodates gradually to the culture it is attempting to conquer, and thereby loses influence over those relatively estranged from that culture. It counts this loss a gain as its own standards shift and as it attracts an increasing number of persons who enjoy the cultural and economic privileges of the society. Though at any given moment of transition the rising sect is associated especially with one economic group, it does not necessarily carry that group as it moves on. There is no indication that classes rise as classes but there is proof that denominations do.[5]

With the development of the church and its succeeding generations, there has come a transition until there is now developing a middle class status and the churches must be careful to not find themselves out of contact with the masses. I would agree with Dr. McGavran that pride develops because of middle class status. Some members are professional people, school teachers, bankers, politicians, and businessmen. The churches must minister to families of the middle class and also reach out to the masses.

Why is it that these traditional church members have moved up in the social classes? There has been emphasis upon Christian teaching in these churches from the beginning. There has also been the guiding precept of a calling for each individual in the church. The Protestant values of frugality, sobriety, work, education, and strict morality have been guiding principals of the Protestants in Brazil. The result of these practices has been the interesting phenomenon of the upward mobility of the churches. However, there has also come the difficulty in relating to the lower classes. Because of this social hiatus the traditional denominations have not experienced the accelerated growth as the Pentecostal denominations have experienced it.

Pope found that as the older denominations proved too
inflexible to meet the needs arising from novel social
situations, that there were new sects that arose to fill in
the gaps.[6] The Pentecostal sects have arisen and are meet-
ing the needs of the migrant Brazilian. The sects range
from the Assembléia de Deus with nearly one million members
to smaller groups within the federation of Pentecostal
churches. The two other largest groups are the Congregação
Cristá no Brasil, and "Brasil para Cristo." These churches
are providing the social prestige that the masses need in
their search for identity.

The migrants from the traditional areas of Brazil have
for the most part been used to the security of the "compadre" and "patrão" system. This security has been cut off
as the migrant has moved to the urban culture.

The "compadre" represents the social structure of his
personal relationships. Graham describes this system in the
following manner:

> Nothing is more characteristic of the patron-dependent
> relationship so typical in Latin America than *compadres-
> co*. A child's godfather is bound not only to the child
> but to the parents by sacred ties almost as strong as
> those that bind the family. In a society where personal
> and primary relationships were all-important and where
> the impersonal connexions of a money economy were not yet
> widespread, the choice of a *compadre* could make or break
> one's life. The large landowner or most prominent
> village citizen would be the first choice of all those
> further down the social scale, and, if he agreed to this
> relationship, he became the protector and guardian angel.
> The whole paternalistic structure was thereby streng-
> thened since the worker did not depend on his own ability
> but relied on this personal tie, a connexion which was
> sustained and perpetuated by his loyalty and subservi-
> ence.[7]

The migrant must be willing to suffer the consequences of
anonymity for the advantages of the "better life" offered in
an industrial society. He must be willing to leave behind
the extended family with its frequent contacts and mutual
help as well as the security of the "patrão" who had been
responsible for him economically.

The adjustment to the urban life style is made easier for
the migrant when he discovers the warmth of the sect or
church that is prepared to seek him out of the crowd.

The loyalty which is inherent in the traditional society
to the family and employer is not quickly lost in the urban
society. Following conversion this characteristic loyalty
is quickly invested in the new life-style found in the Protestant church. It is satisfying activity directed toward
reaching people in similar circumstances which they have
experienced.

The Pentecostal sects have found the urban situation an opportunity for outreach and interaction with the masses of people. There are street meetings conducted in order to get to the people who are too inhibited to come on their own initiative to the churches. These meetings also provide an outlet for the expression of the natural talent and inclination of the Brazilian for oratory and the expression of his emotions. He has the further motivation of his religious experience to cause him to want to relate to the migrant population that has been pulled to the urban milieu.

The assurance of rapid Protestant church growth does not come from the developing of a great industrial park. In this I would agree with Dr. McGavran. However, it is reasonable to believe that industrialization has been catalytic in its effect upon the phenomenal growth of the church in Brazil. The Pentecostal sects have found that their methods of proclaiming the Gospel are adapted to the environment of the industrial park.

The traditional churches of Brazil will not experience t the rapid growth of the Pentecostal churches until there are major functional-structural changes. There must be a willingness on the part of the laity of these churches to become activists and participators in outreach and interaction with the swelling current of rural migrants who have broken with the traditional patterns of their lives. There must also be a willingness among the clergy of the churches to accept the cooperation of the awakened membership to the opportunity of church growth. The laity must be orientated in methods for reaching the reticent middle classes and the more open lower classes. Changes need to be made in order to reach the masses.

The pattern of rapid church growth is not going to deaccelerate in the next ten years. The rate of population growth for the country is 3.2 per cent. The expected urbanization figure for 1980 is sixty per cent of the Brazilian population inhabiting the cities of Brazil. This means that the present pattern of rural-urban migration to the industrialized cities will offer continued opportunity for Protestant church growth.

Brazilian society has had an established pattern of migration during its history. It has been voluntary from the beginning, with the exceptions of the forced migrations from the Northeast during times of flood and drought in the hinterland. Among those who follow this pattern of migration are the Protestants. They are, in fact, known to be more easily drawn to areas of potential economic gain. This willingness to migrate in the hope of better economic conditions could be related both to culture and to the force of Protestantism which emphasizes the necessity of work to properly provide for one's family and the advancement of the cause of the church. Through these migrations the rapid church growth of the industrial areas will be reflected in the emerging opportunity areas of Brazil. Some of these areas have been indicated as the states of Goiá, southern Mato Grosso, and the western part of São Paulo. This is expected as a result of the installation of the Urubupungá hydroelectric facilities on the Paraná River. Other areas are in the rapidly industrializing areas of the south around Porto Alegre, and of the east in the Belo Horizonte section to the state of Espirito Santo along the Rio Dolce. The northeast will also provide an opportunity for rapid church growth resulting from increasing industrialization.

The Brazilian society will be affected by secularization just as all other developed nations of the world have been affected. However, this pattern of secularization will be slower in reaching into Brazil. The typical expression of "Se Deus quiser" (If God wills) would be extremely difficult to sweep out of the Brazilian mind. Brazil will become a secular culture with time, but it will not be soon. The upper classes have been in the process of secularizing since the middle of the nineteenth century. This is not to imply that the growth of the Protestant church in Brazil need be adversely affected by secularization. Dr. McGavran illustrates this generalization by using the rapid growth of the Southern Baptist denomination in Southern California as an example of rapid church growth in a secular society.

From this study it is clear that Brazilian society is the scene of radical culture changes. These range from the primary social relationships to the recreational habits of the Brazilians. Innovations have been stimulated by the patterns of the *fazenda* and the subsistence levels of life for the masses have been radically changed by the rise of industry. Urban planning is an outstanding effect of the causal influence of industrialization. The two primate cities of Brazil have been forced to plan for the urban explosion caused by industry stimulating the influx of the masses. Regional industrial centers have also done this. Housing for the urban dwellers is a major concern of the government. The construction industry is a major employer for the unskilled labor that is flooding into the cities lured by the promise of the "better life" of the industrial parks. If industrial employment is not available for the migrant as a result of his lack of skill or educational qualifications, then there is employment in urban construction programs or, in the case of São Paulo, the building of the subway system.

Just as industrialization has acted as the causal agent in the rapid and radical innovations in the socioeconomic patterns of Brazil, industrialization has acted as a catalyst for the stimulation of Protestant church growth. There could have been additional decades of insignificant Protestant church growth in Brazil if industrialization had not arisen to stimulate the proper conditions for growth. These conditions include the provision for socioeconomic independence and the opportunity to freely participate in the religious plurality of modern culture.

Protestant denominations in Brazil, and particularly the lay-oriented Pentecostal sects, have been rewarded for their activities among the migrants to the industrializaed areas by experiencing accelerated church growth. Industrialization has precipitated cultural innovations which have opened to an increasing number of Brazilians the option of the Protestant church. Openness to change on the part of the newly arrived migrants to the industrial cities, coupled with the reaching out activity of the Protestants results in rapid Protestant church growth in Brazil.

BIBLIOGRAPHY

Books

Azevedo, Fernando de. *A Cidade e o Campo na Civilização Industrial, e Outros Estudos*. Sao Paulo: Edições Melhoramentos, 1962.

_____. *Brazilian Culture*. Trans. by William Rex Crawford. New York: The MacMillan Co., 1950.

Azevedo, Thales de. *Social Change in Brazil*. Gainesville: University of Florida Press, 1963.

Baklanoff, Eric N., Ed. *Colloquium on the Modernization of Brazil*. Baton Rouge: Louisiana State University, 1969.

_____. *New Perspectives of Brazil*. Nashville: University Press, 1966.

Bishop, Elizabeth and Editors of Life. *Life World Library Brazil*. New York: Time Incorporated, 1967.

Eisenstadt, S. N., Ed. *The Protestant Ethic and Modernization--A Comparative View*. New York: Basic Books, Inc., 1968.

Fagg, John Edwin. *Latin America--A General History*. New York: The MacMillan Company, 1963.

Freyre, Gilberto. *The Mansions and the Shanties--The Making of Modern Brazil*. Translated by Harriet de Onis. New York: Knopf, 1963.

_____. *The Masters and the Slaves--A Study in the Development of Brazilian Society*. Translated by Samuel Putnam. New York: Knopf, 1956.

_____. *New World in the Tropics*. New York: Knopf,

Graham, Richard. *Britain and the Onset of Modernization in Brazil, 1850-1914.* Cambridge: Cambridge University Press, 1968.

Hauser, Philip Morris. *Urbanization in Latin America.* New York: International Document Service, 1961.

Heath, Dwight B., Ed. *Contemporary Cultures and Societies of Latin America.* New York: Random House, 1965.

Horowitz, Irving Louis. *Revolution in Brazil--Politics and Society in a Developing Nation.* New York: E. P. Dutton and Company, Inc., 1964.

Ianni, Octavio. *Crisis in Brazil.* New York: Colombia University Press, 1970.

_____. *Racas and Classes Sociais No Brasil.* Rio de Janeiro: Editora Civilizacao Brasileira, S. A., 1966.

Instituto Brasileiro de Estatística. *Anuário Estatístico do Brasil.* Rio de Janeiro: Fundação IBGE, 1968.

_____. (Serviço Nacional da Recensamento). *Atlas--Censitário Industrial do Brasil* Rio de Janeiro: Fundação IBGE, 1965.

_____. (Instituto Brasileiro de Geografia, Departamento de Geografia). *Divisão do Brasil em Micro-Regiões Homogeneas.* Rio de Janeiro: Fundacao IBGE, 1970.

Kahl, Joseph A. *The Measurement of Modernism--A Study of Values in Brazil and Mexico.* Austin: University of Texas, 1968.

Keith, Henry H. and Edwards, S. F., Eds. *Conflict and Continuity in Brazilian Society.* Columbia, South Carolina: University of South Carolina Press, 1969.

Kidder, D. P. and Fletcher, J. C. *Brazil and the Brazilians.* Childs and Peterson, 1857.

Lamego, Alberto Ribeiro. *O Homem e a Serra.* 2d ed. Lucas, Estado de Guanabara: Instituto Brasileiro de Estatísticas, 1963.

Lima, Miguel Alves de. *Novo Paisagens do Brasil.* Rio de Janeiro: Instituto Brasileiro de Estatísticas, 1968.

McGavran, Donald A. *Understanding Church Growth.* Grand Rapids: Wm. B. Eerdmans, 1970.

Mitzman, Arthur. *The Iron Cage: An Historical Interpretation of Max Weber.* New York: Knopf, 1969.

Moog, Vianna. *Bandeirantes and Pioneers*. Translated by L. L. Barrett. New York: George Braziller, 1969.

Nabuco, J. T. *A Statement of the Laws of Brazil*. 3d ed. Washington, D. C.: Pan American Union, 1966.

Pope, Liston. *Millhands and Preachers*. New Haven: Yale University Press, 1942.

Poppino, Rollie E. *Brazil, the Land and People*. London: Oxford University Press, 1968.

Potsch, Waldemiro. *Brazil, Land and People*. Rio de Janeiro: Fundação Alfredo Herculano Xavier Potsch, 1960.

Prado, Caio, Jr. *The Colonial Background of Modern Brazil*. Translated by Suzette Macedo. Berkeley: University of California Press, 1969.

Read, William R. *New Patterns of Church Growth in Brazil*. Grand Rapids: W. B. Eerdmans, 1965.

_____; Monterroso, Victor M.; Johnson, Harmon A. *Latin American Church Growth*. Grand Rapids: William B. Eerdmans, 1969.

Rodriques, Jose Honorio. *The Brazilians: Their Character and Aspirations*. Translated by Ralph Edward Dimajek. Austin: University of Texas Press, 1967.

Rogers, Everett M. *Modernization Among Peasants*. New York: Holt, Rinehart and Winston, Inc., 1969.

Schlesinger, Hugo. *O Brasil Não Pode Parar: Panorama e Desenvolvimento do Indústria Nacional*. Rio de Janeiro: Andes, 1954.

Smith, T. Lynn. *Brazil, People and Institutions*. Baton Rouge: Louisiana State University Press, 1963.

Tippett, Alan R. *Church Growth and the Word of God*. Grand Rapids: William B. Eerdmans Publishing Co., 1970.

Troeltsch, Ernst. *The Social Teaching of the Christian Churches*, Volume I. Translated by Olive Wyon. New York: The MacMillan Co., 1931.

Veliz, Claudio. *Obstacles (to Change in Latin America)*. New York: Oxford Paperback, 1969.

Wagley, Charles. *An Introduction to Brazil*. New York: Columbia University Press, 1963.

Weber, Max. *The Protestant Ethic and the Spirit of Capitalism*. New York: Charles Scribner's Sons, 1958.

Willems, Emilio. *Followers of the New Faith*. Nashville: Vanderbilt University Press, 1967.

Yinger, J. Milton. *Religion, Society and the Individual*. 6th ed. New York: The MacMillan Company, 1957.

Articles and Periodicals

Bazzanella, Waldemiro. "Industrialização e Urbanização no Brasil," *America Latina*, VI, January-March, 1963.

Hutchinson, Bertram. "Urban Social Mobility Rates in Brazil Related to Migration and Changing Occupational Structure," *America Latina*, VI (July-September, 1963), 123.

Melo Filho, Maurilo. "The Brazil of the Seventies," *Manchete*, I, 1970.

Morse, Richard M. "Trends and Issues in Urban Research," *Latin American Research Review*, VI (Spring, 1971), p. 228.

Toledo, Caio de. "Brazil: An Underdeveloped Giant Wakes Up," *Student World*, LVII (First Quarter, 1964), 41-52.

Young, Lewis H., Ed. "Booming Brazil Finds a Key to Growth," *Business Week*, March 13, 1971, pp. 90-93.

Bulletins

Embaixada do Brasil. "Centro Industrial de Aratú," *Boletim Especial*, LXXIV (April, 1971), p. 1.

Wilkening, E. A. "Comparison of Migrants in Two Rural and an Urban Area of Central Brazil," A Report Supported by the Land Tenure Center. November, 1968, p. 36.

Unpublished Material

MARC. "Brief Explanation of the Brazil Church Growth Computer Project." World Vision International, Monrovia, California, 1967.

_____. "Continuing Evangelism in Brazil." Missions Advanced Research and Communication Center, Monrovia, California, 1971.

Voalkel, J. W. "Evangelical Christians and the Middle Class in Latin America." School of Missions, Fuller Theological Seminary, December, 1970.

Other Sources

Leeds, Anthony. "Urbanization in Brazil." Class Lecture by
     Visiting Professor of Anthropology at University of
     Texas given at University of California at Los
     Angeles, May 5, 1971.

Ineson, Frank A. Personal Interview. May 5, 1971.

McGavran, Donald A. Personal Interview. May 5, 1971.

Read, William R. Personal Interview. May 5, 1971.

APPENDIX

QUESTIONÁRIO

Estamos fazendo um estudo dos efeitos da industrialização no crescimento da igreja evangélica no Brazil. Faça-nós o favor de preencher as respostas destas perguntas nós espaços em branco.

I. HISTÓRICO ESPÍRITUAL

 1. Nome _____

 2. Data que tornou-se membro duma igreja evangélica

    _____ Qual igreja? _____

 3. A idade quando aceitou Cristo como seu Salvador __

 4. A cidade onde foi convertido _____

 5. A sua família sempre foi participantes nas festas

    religiósas da paróquia? Sim ___ Não ___

    Quase sempre ___

 6. Indique uma ou duas destas _____

 7. Em que maneira o senhor recebeu o seu primeiro
    convite para assistir uma igreja evangélica?
    Através:

    (1) companheiro de serviço _____

    (2) vizinho   _____

    (3) desconhecido   _____

    (4) folheto   _____

    (5) cartaz de aviso   _____

    (6) rádio   _____

    (7) outro   _____

 8. O senhor assistiu o seu primeiro culto numa casa

    particular? _____ ou num templo? _____ Qual? ____

 9. O senhor sente-se que sua vida tornou-se mais
    abundante e feliz depois de tornar-se um membro
    da igreja evangélica?

    Sim _____ Não _____ Não tenho certeza _____

II. HISTÓRIA DA MUDÂNCA

    10. A populaçao da sua terra natal foi:

        (1)   0 a   300 pessoas _____

        (2) 300 a   500 pessoas _____

        (3) 500 a 1000 pessoas _____

        (4) 1000 a 5000 pessoas _____

    11. A razão que saiu da sua terra natal:

        (1) oportunidade limitada de serviço _____

        (2) oportunidade limitada de estudar _____

        (3) um amigo ou parente que já mudou-se para a
            cidade me influenciou _____

        (4) a cidade ofereceu uma vida melhor para mim e
            minha família _____

    12. Partiu da sua terra natal pela estrada de ferro
        _____ ônibus _____ caminhão _____ outro _____

    13. Quando partiu da sua terra natal a estrada era
        de: terra _____ pedra _____ concreta _____
        asfalto _____

    14. Na sua terra natal morava numa casa de:
        madeira _____ tijolo _____ outra _____

    15. A distância da sua terra natal a sua cidade é
        mais ou menos quantos kilómetros? _____

    16. Logo que chegou na cidade morava numa casa de
        madeira _____ tijolo _____ outra _____

    17. Quanto tempo o senhor morava na sua primeira
        residência antes de mudar-se?

        (1) 6 meses _____

        (2) 1 ano _____

        (3) 2 anos _____

(4) outro _____ (indique)

18. Qual foi sua idade quando partiu da sua terra natal para a cidade? _____

III. EMPRÊGO INDUSTRIAL

19. Quando chegou na cidade encontrou qual tipo de serviço?

(1) na fábrica _____

(2) jardineiro _____

(3) representante _____

(4) prefeito _____

(5) outro _____ (indique)

20. Quanto tempo levou para obter um emprêgo industrial?

(1) 6 meses _____

(2) outro _____ (indique)

21. Qual tipo de artigo foi produzido na indústria onde o senhor primeiramente encontrou serviço?

automóvel _____ tinta _____ outra _____

22. Acha que a cidade lhe ofereceu uma vida melhor financeiramente do que sua terra natal teria lhe oferecida?

Sim _____ Não _____ Não tenho certeza _____

IV. CRESCIMENTO DA IGREJA

23. Sua igreja está aumentando?

Sim _____ Não _____ Não tenho certeza _____

24. Da sua própria experiência, acha mais fácil a convidar os vizinhos recém-chegados na cidade para assistir os cultos ou é mais fácil convidar seus vizinhos que sempre moravam na cidade?

_____

25. Quantos pentecostais o senhor conhece no seu

    lugar de serviço? _____

26. Quantos Presbyterianos, Methodistas e/ou Batistas

    o senhor conhece no seu lugar de serviço? _____

27. Acha que um evangélico de convicções de honesti-
    dade e serviço sério havera possíbilidade de sus-
    tentar cada vez mais sua igreja e seu programa de
    evangelização?

    Sim _____ Não _____ Não tenho certeza _____

28. Quantos membros da sua igreja trabalham na

    fábrica?

    (1) 1 - 25% _____

    (2) 25 - 50% _____

    (3) 50 - 75% _____

    (4) over 75% _____

QUESTIONNAIRE FOR PERSONAL INTERVIEWS

1. In what ways do you find that industrialization in Latin America is affecting its culture? In what way or ways do you find that Brazil has been affected by industrialization?

2. Do you find that rapid Protestant church growth is always or nearly always related to the phenomenon of industrialization? Is it valid to expect rapid church growth in Latin America in areas of expanding industrial activity?

3. Do you believe that there will be increasingly accelerated church growth in Brazil as the traditional areas, e.g., the northeast, become modernized and industrialized?

4. Where could one expect the greatest Protestant church growth to be in Brazil during the next ten years? Why do you foresee a rapid growth in these areas?

5. Do you believe the traditional, e.g., historic, Protestant denominations in Brazil are evangelizing as effectively as possible among the migrants? For example, are they serving as effectively as possible among the migrants to the city of São Paulo?

6. Is it reasonable to hold that the Pentecostal sects in Brazil are definitely encouraged in their growth by the developing of a great industrial park?

7. Could the historic denominations grow as rapidly as the Pentecostal groups in Brazil without major functional-structural modifications?

8. When could the present rate of rapid Protestant church growth in Brazil be expected to deaccelerate?

9. Do you believe that the pattern of rapid church growth in the highly industrialized areas of Brazil will eventually be reflected in other areas?

10. In what way or ways would you understand the pattern of secularization of the Western industrial culture to affect the growth of the Protestant church in Brazil?

11. What kind of church growth can be expected in an area of high mobility? Is there reason to believe that a great influx of people can be expected in the church if as many as four-fifths of those living in the area are planning to move to another area?

The author, the Reverend Charles W. Gates, is a
native of Ohio. He married the former Roma Joanne Perry
in 1950 while they were students of Olivet Nazarene
College. Mr. Gates received his undergraduate degree
from Olivet in 1952. He received a B.D. from the Nazarene Theological Seminary in Kansas City, Missouri in the
spring of 1955. Before leaving for Brazil, Mr. Gates
served the Canaan Hill Church of the Nazarene in Lawson
Missouri (1954-1956) and was the first pastor of the Avon
Lake Church of the Nazarene during the years 1956 to 1958.
It was during this latter period that the Gates received
their call to Brazil, and were one of the first families
sent to Brazil by the General Board of the Church of the
Nazarene. While there Mr. Gates was instrumental in the
opening of the Nazarene Mission in the state of Minas
Gerais. He served as Mission Treasurer during his first
two terms and from 1967 to 1970 was the director of the
Seminario e Instituto Biblico da Igreja do Nazarene in
Campinas, Sao Paulo. The Gates have one son, Gregory Lee.